Débarrassée d'entraves mieux
qu'auparavant la maison des
hommes maîtresse de sa forme
s'installe dans la nature.
        Entière en soi
faisant son affaire de tout sol

dansent la Terre et le Soleil
la danse des quatre saisons
la danse de l'année
la danse des jours de
vingt-quatre heures
le sommet et le gouffre des
solstices
la plaine des équinoxes

Sa valeur est en ceci : le corps humain choisi comme support admissible des nombres.

... Voilà la proportion la proportion qui met de l'ordre dans nos rapports avec l'alentour.

Pourquoi pas ? Peu nous chaut en cette matière l'avis de la baleine de l'aigle des rochers ou celui de l'abeille.

CONTENTS

LE CORBUSIER
ARCHITECT, PAINTER, POET
Jean Jenger

DISCOVERIES
HARRY N. ABRAMS, INC., PUBLISHERS

Paris 1887. The construction of a 300-metre (984-foot) high tower was begun on the esplanade of the Champ de Mars. The Eiffel Tower would soon be a household name all over the world. On 6 October, Charles-Edouard Jeanneret, not yet known as Le Corbusier, was born in La Chaux-de-Fonds in the Swiss canton of Neuchâtel, a few kilometres from the French border.

CHAPTER 1

BOYHOOD AND YOUTH IN THE JURA

In his drawings and watercolours, Charles-Edouard Jeanneret returned constantly to the scenery of his childhood. The important place he gave in his work to the natural world, throughout his life, certainly originated in his childhood experience of the Jura (opposite, c. 1905). Right: a drawing of a crow.

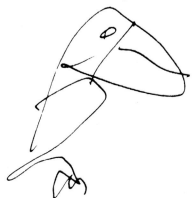

La Chaux-de-Fonds is a small town perched at a height of about one thousand metres (over three thousand feet) in the harsh climate of the Swiss Jura. In 1887 it had a population of 27,000 and most of its industrial activity was devoted to watchmaking. Charles-Edouard Jeanneret's father, like his father before him, was a watch-face enameller. His ancestors on his father's side came from the south-west of France to the mountains around Neuchâtel to escape from the wars of religion. Charles-Edouard's mother, Charlotte Marie Amélie Perret, was a keen pianist. Under her influence Charles-Edouard's brother, Albert, who was two years older than him, would become a musician. Some of his mother's family lived in Belgium and it was from the name of one of her ancestors, Le Corbésier, that in 1920 Charles-Edouard created the pseudonym which he used first for his articles and books, later for his sculpture and his architecture. He often played with this pseudonym, linking it to the French word for crow (*corbeau*) and using the sketched outline of the bird as a signature.

The art school in La Chaux-de-Fonds specialized in training its students to design and decorate watchcases. Charles-Edouard became a skilled engraver: in 1906 he won a prize with an engraved watchcase (left) at the Milan exhibition. His early themes, natural forms from the surrounding Jura countryside, soon ceased to be purely representational (opposite above, *Flowers and Leaves*). His teacher, L'Eplattenier, believed his students should look for the basic structure and organization in things before using their forms in a creative manner. Below: Charles-Edouard Jeanneret (right) with his friend Léon Perrin (left). Opposite below: Charles-Edouard (on the pedestal), his brother Albert and their parents in 1889.

Charles-Edouard's father was the president of his local branch of the Alpine Club and was a passionate mountain climber. He passed on his enthusiasm for the forests, valleys and peaks of the Jura to his son at an early age.

As a boy Charles-Edouard was an able student who showed little interest in the piano but was often to be found drawing. At the age of thirteen, when he had completed his general education, he enrolled in the art school in La Chaux-de-Fonds, which specialized in the decorative arts and watch engraving.

Art school: an outstanding teacher

Charles L'Eplattenier was to play a decisive role in shaping the young Charles-Edouard's future. He was just twenty-six and had recently returned from his studies at the Ecole Nationale des Beaux-Arts in Paris. Himself a painter with a deep appreciation of the natural world, he used to take his students on drawing expeditions to the woodlands and meadows of the Jura.

L'Eplattenier became principal of the art school in 1903 and guided the teaching towards a kind of naturalism, akin to Art Nouveau, a movement which, in the late 19th century, searched for a style

that avoided all historical and academic influences.
Art Nouveau soon swept across the whole of Europe,
thanks partly to the growing number of art magazines.
Emile Gallé and Hector Guimard in France,
William Morris in England, Victor Horta in
Belgium, Antoni Gaudí in Spain were some of
its most brilliant exponents before Charles Rennie
Mackintosh in Glasgow, Josef Hoffmann and Otto
Wagner in Vienna, Henry Van de Velde and Peter
Behrens in Germany toned down its excesses, and
began the transition towards the modern movement.

Born at the turning-point of the 19th and 20th
centuries, the young Charles-Edouard Jeanneret was
deeply influenced by the teaching of L'Eplattenier,
whom he held in great affection. Later experiences
transformed the young man's personality.
The naturalism inculcated at the art school in
La Chaux-de-Fonds disappeared very rapidly from
his work, but the influence of the natural world
remained engraved on his spirit, and on his aims
and methods, for the rest of his life.

Villa Fallet, his first building

Jeanneret was drawn towards painting, but met with
opposition from L'Eplattenier who tried to discourage
him. 'One of my teachers (a very remarkable man)

Charles L'Eplattenier
played an
important role as
Charles-Edouard
Jeanneret's teacher
and mentor. He found
work for his student
with René Chapallaz,
a local architect,
with whom Jeanneret
collaborated on three
building projects: the
Fallet, Jaquemet and
Stotzer villas. Villa
Fallet (below) is
strongly rooted in the
'picturesque' tradition.
Jeanneret's contribution
is difficult to identify,
but decorations
based on a
stylized fir-
tree shape,
plus the use
of colour
in the
gables are
attributed
to him.

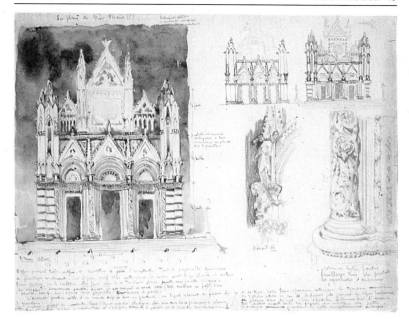

gently dissuaded me from the choice of a mediocre career. He wanted to turn me into an architect. I loathed architecture and architects.... As I was only sixteen, I accepted his verdict and obeyed his edict: I took up architecture.' He joined the advanced course in art and design set up by L'Eplattenier in 1905 for the teaching of architecture and decoration. During the two years he was to spend on the course he had the opportunity to carry out his first architectural project, commissioned by Louis Fallet, a master engraver and one of the governors of the art school.

The Italian tour

Charles-Edouard felt the need to broaden his horizons. In 1907 he decided to use the money he had earned for his work on the Villa Fallet to make his first long journey. With his friend Léon Perrin, a sculpture student, he went to Tuscany, about which L'Eplattenier had so often spoken, spending a month in Florence. Through his drawings he tried to go beyond form and

At the turn of the century the 'Italian Tour' was still an accepted requirement for the study of art or architecture. Charles L'Eplattenier often told his students about his own experiences on one. In September 1907 Charles-Edouard Jeanneret and Léon Perrin set out on a trip lasting nearly two months; it took them to Pisa, Siena (above, the cathedral), and Florence, then to Ravenna, Bologna, Verona, Padua and Venice. Jeanneret discovered new architectural styles, light and colour.

decoration, forcing himself to decipher the organization and logic of the architecture he saw. 'I set down my impressions in my notebook every day; it's a jumble of impressions that could be very useful to me one day. Later I read it over again and add my corrections and it helps me to remember things better.' He wrote twenty or so letters to his parents, and five detailed accounts of his trip to his teacher, describing his visits and his discoveries. Throughout his life he enjoyed the discipline of writing.

Even when he was very young, he was devoted to reading, broadening his mind through the discovery of history, philosophy and poetry. Henri Provensal's *L'Art de demain*, John Ruskin's *Seven Lamps of Architecture* (1849) and *Mornings in Florence* (1875), Eugène Grasset's *Méthode de composition ornementale* (1905), Owen Jones' *Grammar of Ornament* (1856) and Hippolyte-Adolphe Taine's *Voyage en Italie* (1864) influenced his thought and work for years.

From Vienna to Paris

From Florence, Charles-Edouard Jeanneret went on to Ravenna, Bologna, Verona and Venice, then to Budapest and Vienna, where he spent the winter and where he

In letters to his parents, and accounts of his trip to his teacher, Jeanneret analysed his impressions and described the work he was doing. He made notes in his guidebook, the famous Baedeker, and produced many drawings, plans, sketches, notes and watercolours (above, a view of Fiesole) in the notebooks and sketchpads he had with him. He made a particular study of the dimensions of buildings in an effort to understand their proportions; often scribbled in the margin, beside the drawings, are his notes, the searchings of a young mind, eager to reach a new understanding of the world and architecture.

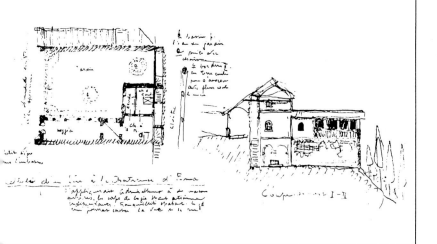

worked briefly for Josef Hoffmann. From Vienna he
travelled to Nuremburg, Munich, Strasbourg, Nancy
and Paris where, with the small amount of money still
remaining to him, he rented an attic in the Rue des
Ecoles. There he met Frantz Jourdain, president of
the Salon d'Automne, who designed the first
of the Samaritaine department stores, using
almost entirely iron and glass; he also met
Henri Sauvage, who designed the terraced
blocks of flats clad in white tiling that were
built shortly afterwards in Rue Vavin. On a
trip to Lyons he was introduced to the young
architect Tony Garnier, whose work on 'the
industrial city' greatly interested him.

During a second trip to Paris in 1908 he
visited the graphic artist Eugène Grasset,
who introduced him to the Perret brothers.
Like other pioneers of reinforced concrete,
including François Hennebique, Anatole
de Baudot and Coignet in France, and
Ernest Leslie Ransome in the USA, Auguste,
Gustave and Claude Perret were endeavouring
to discover the full range of structural and
sculptural capabilities of this new material.

The Carthusian
monastery at Ema,
near Florence (above)
was a high point of the
trip. Below: the citadel
at Nuremberg.

Although their biggest projects had not yet been constructed – the Théâtre des Champs-Elysées of 1911–3, the Hôtel du Mobilier National (the repository of the state collections of furniture) of 1934 and the Musée des Travaux Publics of 1937 – the Perrets had already shown their exceptional mastery of reinforced concrete in their block of flats in the Rue Franklin (1903) and their garage in the Rue de Ponthieu (1905).

The office of the brothers Perret

Charles-Edouard Jeanneret spent fourteen months from 1908 to 1909 working in the Perrets' office. Here he discovered the possibilities of reinforced concrete, as well as a new approach to architectural construction. He came to realize that architecture must resolve in a logical manner the problems created when new technical solutions to domestic needs become available. He became more

The work of Le Corbusier has often been contrasted with the work of his employer, Auguste Perret: the 'modernism' of the first versus the 'academicism' of the second. Their concepts of the window are radically different, Perret advocating vertical windows that (in his view) echo the shape of the human body and provide light right to the back of the room; Le Corbusier championing horizontal windows that give a panoramic view out and light up the corners inside. In 1924 Le Corbusier sketched Perret in front of a 'ribbon window'.

and more aware of the limitations of the formalist ideas taught at the art school in La Chaux-de-Fonds. In a long letter to his teacher L'Eplattenier, written on 22 November 1908, he explained his discoveries and his doubts. 'When I arrived in Paris I felt a great emptiness inside me, and I said to myself, "Poor thing! You don't know anything yet and, worse still, you don't know what it is you don't know." That was what caused me such bitter anxiety…. My studies of the Romanesque persuaded me that architecture is not simply about harmony of form…it was something else…but what? I wasn't sure.'

The period spent in the Perret office marked a crucial phase in the transformation of Jeanneret's personality. 'It was the Perret brothers who spurred me on.' As well as working part-time in their office, he also continued to satisfy his continual thirst for knowledge. He read texts by the influential Gothic Revival architect Eugène-Emmanuel Viollet-le-Duc and absorbed his ideas on the structural requirements of buildings. He took courses at the Ecole des Beaux-Arts and the Sorbonne, read in the Bibliothèque Nationale and the Bibliothèque Sainte-Geneviève, visited museums again and again and spent hours clambering over the high parts of Notre Dame.

Although they disagreed at times, Auguste Perret and Le Corbusier had a mutual respect that did not diminish. When Perret later visited the site of Le Corbusier's *Unité d'habitation* apartment building in Marseilles, he revealed the importance he attached to both himself and to Le Corbusier: 'There are two architects in France and the other one is Le Corbusier'.

Reinforced concrete goes back to the 19th century but architects were restrained in their use of it. In 1903 the Perret brothers built one of the first blocks of flats on a reinforced concrete framework in the Rue Franklin in Paris (above). In spite of the cladding of tiles painted with a floral design, the exposed framework shows the relationship between supports and beams quite clearly.

Charles-Edouard Jeanneret's study trip to Germany in 1910 and his great journey to the East in 1911 transformed the young man's personality. He still felt the need, however, to spend five more years in his native town before he was able to cut himself off from his roots in the Jura and to settle in Paris in 1917. By that time Jeanneret was almost ready to blossom into Le Corbusier.

CHAPTER 2
TRANSFORMATION

A self-portrait of Charles-Edouard Jeanneret (opposite) at the age of thirty, the year he settled in Paris. His eyesight was poor and he gradually lost the sight in one eye almost completely. Here he has not yet adopted the large spectacles that he wore later in life, but he is already wearing a bow-tie, his trademark. Right: sketch of a shell.

Charles-Edouard Jeanneret's spell in the office of the Perret brothers did not immediately free him from the strong cultural ties binding him to La Chaux-de-Fonds. In 1909 he returned to his birthplace. Together with a few friends from the advanced course at the art school he created the Ateliers d'Art Réunis. The aim of the association was to develop art in every area, but it did not succeed and was quickly discontinued. Jeanneret built two villas, Villa Stotzer and Villa Jaquemet; he had already received the commission and begun the plans before he left for Italy. He also sketched out a design for a new building for the art school in La Chaux-de-Fonds, a design that he was to resurrect in his plan for a museum with open-ended potential for growth from 1929 to 1930; this was eventually realized in his design for the Museum of Western Art in Tokyo in 1959.

The trip to Germany

In April 1910 he set out on a extended trip to Germany. The art school in La Chaux-de-Fonds had asked him to write a report on the teaching of arts and crafts in

Charles-Edouard Jeanneret began thinking about the Villas Jaquemet (this page) and Stotzer (opposite) during his holiday in Italy and Austria; he was co-signatory to the plans with René Chapallaz. Although less

Germany, and its relationship with industry. Jeanneret went to a number of different towns in Germany, visiting firms whose products were of artistic as well as industrial interest. His *Etude sur le mouvement d'art en Allemagne* was published in La Chaux-de-Fonds in 1912. He was brilliantly to re-use some of the ideas in 1925, in one of his most important books, *L'Art décoratif d'aujourd'hui*.

The Behrens office

In Berlin, Jeanneret worked in the office of the architect Peter Behrens from October 1910 to March 1911; Walter Gropius and Ludwig Mies van der Rohe were both to work there at a later date. He did not, apparently, find Behrens' style especially avant-garde, but he learned a lot about the organization of a big office and the problems imposed on architecture by industry.

Jeanneret had still not quite completed the transformation begun during his first journey to Italy, his spell in Paris and his most recent trip to Germany. A long journey in 1911 to Central and Eastern Europe, Greece and back to Italy was to be decisive.

exaggerated than the Villa Fallet, they still show a marked tendency towards the picturesque. Their façades govern their interior layout; the idea that 'the design evolves from inside out' has not yet arrived.

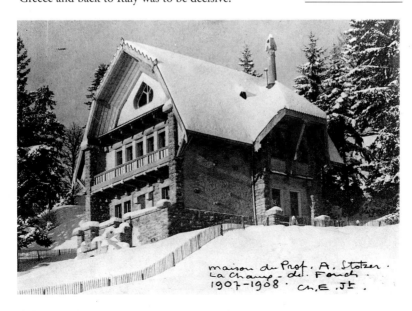

maison du Prof. A. Stotzer.
La Chaux-de-Fonds.
1907-1908. Ch.E.Jt.

The journey to Asia Minor

Jeanneret left Switzerland on 7 May 1911 with his college
friend Auguste Klipstein, an art historian who was
writing a thesis on El Greco. The journey lasted nearly
a year and during it the two friends discovered the
Mediterranean, Eastern Europe and Turkey. For
Jeanneret, brought up in the mountains of the Jura,
it was a shock and a revelation; he was stunned. It was
now that the transformation he had been dreaming
about for years was completed: 'I was not yet a man;
before life opened out in front of me I needed to gain
a personality.'

He repeated the habit he had acquired, during his first
travels, of always carrying a small sketchbook measuring
10 by 17 centimetres (nearly 4 by 6½ inches). He filled
more than eighty of these notebooks during his lifetime,
in black and white and in colour, writing notes, lists and
sums and sketches. More and more notes
and reflections poured out.

'The reason for drawing is to interiorize something one has seen, to make it part of one's personal history. Once things have been absorbed by means of the pencil they remain inside one for life; they are written indelibly, inscribed.' On a regular basis he sent long letters to his parents, who published them in the local newspaper, *La Feuille d'avis de La Chaux-de-Fonds*.

In Serbia, Romania and Bulgaria he studied the vernacular, anonymous architecture of the villages, eager to discover the secret of their response to the human need for shelter.

He stayed at the monastery of Mount Athos in Greece for a week, enthralled in equal measure by the life of the monks, the beauty of the site and the architecture. In Turkey he discovered mosques. He was fascinated by the simple shapes and dazzling whiteness of Mediterranean architecture: 'Volume is governed by a simple geometry: the square, the cube, the sphere.'

This man who had spent his youth in the dark pine forests and misty valleys of the Jura was dazzled by the light.

The Parthenon

The Acropolis was the high point of the long journey. Jeanneret and Klipstein spent several weeks in Athens. The future Le Corbusier passed whole days absorbing

On the trip to Asia Minor three whole weeks were devoted to the Acropolis. Amongst the silent stones Jeanneret found the intense spiritual experience that he was to seek in architecture from that day forward. He measured, calculated and compared until, he proclaimed in a letter to L'Eplattenier, he was thoroughly exhausted. In the Acropolis he found the order that he was to look for increasingly in architecture, and which he considered an essential feature of art. For him, perfection of proportion and form had a moral aspect; Doric moulding held 'morality' or an 'infallible, implacable character; precision'; mouldings expressed 'courage'. Another subject of interest during the trip was rural architecture in Bulgaria (opposite).

In 1911 Jeanneret and Klipstein set off on a long journey. 'With knapsack on my back I traversed countries on foot, on horseback, by boat, by car, observing the diversity of races and the basic uniformity of the human race.' The journey had to satisfy Klipstein's interest in painting and Jeanneret's in architecture. The young art-school student from La Chaux-de-Fonds discovered under the Mediterranean and Near Eastern skies an architecture he had not known existed. He was as interested in peasant architecture and the simplest structures as he was in great monuments and spent time making sketches (here, of Istanbul and the Parthenon). He mixed photography, writing and drawing. He produced plans and drawings, but also wrote reams of notes on the details of construction, decoration, materials and colour. In Istanbul Jeanneret was taken with the mosques, with their strict geometrical proportions based on the square, the cube and the circle.

In 1912 Georges Favre-Jacot, an important figure in the watch-making industry in Neuchâtel and the creator of Zenith timepieces, commissioned Charles-Edouard Jeanneret to build a villa for him at Le Locle, near La Chaux-de-Fonds. This time the architecture departs from the local style: the neo-classical villa probably has its origins in the work of Behrens and Perret, but betrays traces of Mediterranean inspiration as well.

'the straight lines of marble, the vertical columns and the entablatures parallel to the sea's horizon'. Besides the 'skilful, accurate and magnificent interplay of the volumes in the bright light', he hoped to discover the active force behind architecture. He found the beauty and the power of the Parthenon 'the purest creation of the human mind...a machine designed to arouse and disturb'; though physical in essence, it was to an even greater extent spiritual.

Return to La Chaux-de-Fonds

After Naples then Rome, the voyage to Asia Minor ended in November 1911. Jeanneret went back to the Carthusian monastery at Ema near Florence which had made such an impression on him in 1908. He then returned to La Chaux-de-Fonds, where he was to spend five more years before moving permanently to France. After the months spent with the Perret brothers, and after his extended travels, his return to his native town might seem surprising. Did he feel too young, at twenty-five, to leave his family, his teacher L'Eplattenier, his childhood home, his friends from school? Perhaps he had not yet fully completed the transformation begun by his voyages of discovery in the Mediterranean and Asia Minor.

L'Eplattenier was trying to build up a new department in the art school to train artists in modern industrial processes and convinced Jeanneret and two of his former colleagues, Georges Aubert and Léon Perrin, to come and work there. His success was short-lived, however, because Jeanneret had been commissioned to design a number of buildings. In 1912 he built

While Jeanneret was working on plans for the Villa Favre-Jacot, his parents asked him to build a villa for them in a small forest above La Chaux-de-Fonds. The house stands at the top of a sloping garden with a broad terrace at the top. The design is four-square and solid, and remarkable for its meticulous organization. This time 'the design evolves from the inside out': four columns in the centre of the building mark the corners of the ground-floor music room, designed to accommodate his mother's piano. This room determines the layout of the rooms around it. At the west end of the building the central axis terminates in a semi-circular kind of apse which houses the dining room. The house has a white painted stucco finish, unusual in that part of the Jura. It soon became known as 'La Villa Blanche'.

a house for the industrialist Favre-Jacot at Le Locle, near La Chaux-de-Fonds. In 1916 he completed two projects: the Villa Schwob for another industrialist and Villa Jeanneret for his parents.

The reinforced concrete framework of the Villa Schwob consists of sixteen square columns; the

LE PROPRIÉTAIRE :   L'ARCHITECTE :

Anatoly Schwob   CIE Jeanneret

LA CHAUX·DE·FONDS   8 SEPT: 1916 .

ECHELLE 1:50

In his first three houses, Villa Fallet, Villa Stotzer and Villa Jaquemet, Jeanneret had concentrated on the design of the exterior, determining interior organization according to the requirements of the exterior. In the three villas built between 1912 and 1916 the interior plan dictates the exterior. The influence of Frank Lloyd Wright has also been noted; later Jeanneret was also to refer to his 'inclination towards order, organization, and towards a purely architectural creation'.

arrangement of the four major supports in the main drawing room in the centre of the ground floor is similar to that in the Villa Jeanneret; they dictate the rest of the plan. The construction conveys a feeling of austerity and strength and is reminiscent of the Perrets' work. Its whiteness and its severe outline, plus its roof terrace, soon earned it the name 'Villa Turque'.

Dom-ino: a system of construction

Apart from plans for the restoration of the Scala cinema in La Chaux-de-Fonds, Jeanneret now drew up plans for a number of projects that were never realized. He

In February 1912 Jeanneret sent a circular letter to local bankers, industrialists and businessmen claiming to be a specialist in reinforced concrete, although he had so far only used it in traditional ways. The Villa Schwob (left, during construction and opposite, the signed contract) was his first structure in reinforced concrete. He had learned the lessons of Auguste Perret: the arrangement of the upright supports follows the layout of the building and the framework plays an essential part in the final appearance of the house.

became interested in the problems of social housing. When he heard about the first destruction of houses in Flanders after the outbreak of the First World War he started to develop a process of industrialized building using a system of structural modules. These would make it possible to erect houses of any size simply and rapidly; the arrangement of the dwellings would be flexible and the inhabitants could finish the details themselves. Dom-ino, the name given to this system of building, was formed from the root of the Latin word *domus*, house, and the root of the word 'innovation'; it also evokes the game of dominoes in which one piece is joined to another, just as the prefabricated elements of the system would be joined to one another.

Reinforced concrete made it possible to do away with the traditional functions of the walls (supporting floors and ceilings and enclosing the built space). Jeanneret tried to exploit this freedom as much as he could. The basic unit of his Dom-ino system (below) consists of three floors, six vertical columns and a staircase. To make the exterior walls free-standing, the supports are not at the edge and they join the horizontal surfaces smoothly, so that ceilings and walls can be perfectly smooth as well.

As well as his teaching, which soon came to an end, and his work as an architect, Jeanneret continued to draw and to paint. He exhibited sixteen watercolours from his trip to Asia Minor, in an exhibition held in Neuchâtel in 1916 named *Langage des pierres*, and several of the same paintings in the Salon d'Automne in Paris, where he went from time to time. He continued to read the works of historians, art critics and poets, discovering Maurice Denis' *Théories, 1890–1910* (1912) and Auguste Choisy's *Histoire de l'architecture* (1899). He collected his own notes and articles into a *Voyage d'Orient*, but the book was not published until 1966. Furthermore, he embarked upon the editing of a book on the construction of cities, but the text was never published.

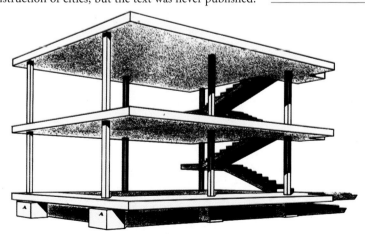

Le Corbusier remained faithful to the reinforced concrete framework, columns and floors. He used variations of the Domino system in many projects for mass-produced housing

Departure from La Chaux-de-Fonds

In 1917 Jeanneret was thirty. At this stage he had already built six villas in La Chaux-de-Fonds and Le Locle, and had established his reputation with several well-to-do local families, so he could have pursued a successful career as an architect in the area. However, he had a feeling that if he stayed there he would not find the scope that he required; he wanted a wider range of opportunities and also a wider circle of contacts. As an intellectual and artistic centre, Paris attracted him. He uprooted himself at last from La Chaux-de-Fonds and moved permanently to France.

Jeanneret had reached the end of this first long period of his life; over those last ten years or so, after a modest education, he had, thanks to his burning intellectual curiosity and through his travels, his encounters and his reading, accumulated a whole new store of knowledge.

A largely self-taught man, he never stopped making notes, drawing and writing, always aspiring to a clearer understanding of the meaning of life and the significance of objects and architecture. Gradually he was able to evolve a concept of harmony, of architecture and of the function of the architect that diverged from the one he had been taught in La Chaux-de-Fonds. Le Corbusier was soon to emerge from the chrysalis of Charles-Edouard Jeanneret.

(above). Several of the 'five points of the new architecture' (published 1927) were drawn from this system. The Citrohan house (1920) and the luxury apartments 'immeuble villas' (1922) are based on variants of the system, whose principles reappear throughout his architectural career, from the white villas of the 1920s to the large edifices of Chandigarh.

In the garden of the Villa Jeanneret in La Chaux-de-Fonds stand the Jeannerets – Charles-Edouard (left), his brother Albert (right) and their parents.

From 1917 Charles-Edouard Jeanneret (who assumed the name Le Corbusier as an author from 1920, as an architect from 1922 and as a painter from 1928) continued to develop his ideas and his professional skills. Whether he was engaged in sculpture, painting, or architecture, in town planning or in writing, the twenty years that followed were exceptionally productive.

CHAPTER 3
FLOWERING

The banker Raoul La Roche had a fine collection of Cubist and Purist paintings. The villa built for him by Jeanneret was designed to meet the requirements of a man who lived alone, and who needed a gallery to hang his pictures. Right: sketch of Corbusier's 'open-hand' motif.

When he arrived in Paris in 1917, Jeanneret moved to 20 Rue Jacob, not far from the church of Saint-Germain-des-Prés. He stayed there until 1934, when he and his wife moved to the penthouse flat of an apartment block he had just completed in Rue Nungesser et Coli, on the edge of Paris and the Boulogne district. He had married Yvonne Gallis in December 1930, three months after becoming a naturalized Frenchman.

Meanwhile, in 1924 he opened his architectural practice with his cousin Pierre Jeanneret at 35 Rue de Sèvres. It was their habit for both partners to sign the plans that were produced by the practice, until their separation in 1940. They started working together again in 1951 on important commissions from the government of India.

Le Corbusier the industrialist

Until 1920, Jeanneret was unable to find regular, well-paid work. He worked first in a research office, set up to study the applications of reinforced concrete. Next he became director of a company that made bricks and building materials, but the company failed. He then set up his own consultancy, the Société d'Entreprise Industrielle et d'Etudes (the Society for Industrial Development and

In the perspective drawings below (showing the Loucheur house and standardized housing), Le Corbusier depicts the interior space rather than the walls or partitions enclosing it.

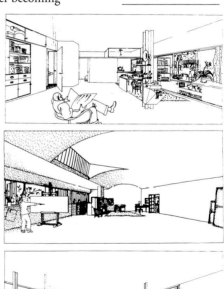

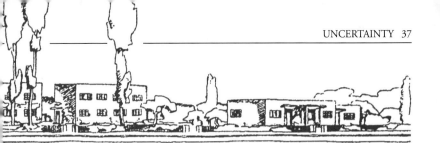

Studies), within which he invented a certain number of new processes and construction materials.

In 1919 he designed the Monol houses, constructed from fibrocement with a vaulted roof, repeating the same design principle in the Petite Maison at La Celle-Saint-Cloud, and, later in the 1950s, in the Jaoul and the Sarabhai houses. He began to consider the problems of low-cost workers' housing. He was interested in what the American efficiency engineer Frederick Winslow Taylor had achieved and tried to think of ways of rationalizing the construction process along industrial lines. Though evidently gaining satisfaction and pride from his position as company manager, he did not possess the requisite business skills. In the end, at a time of recession when building activity in France was much reduced, his ventures met with no success at all.

Project (never built) for houses in rough-cast concrete (1919); they were to have been constructed on a gravel bank, using gravel quarried on the spot, mixed with lime and poured into moulds 40 cm (over 15 inches) deep. 'The straight line is the great achievement of modern architecture. We must clean the cobwebs of romanticism from our minds.'

Yvonne Gallis, Le Corbusier's wife, had been a model in Monaco. She gave him great stability, helping him to pick up the pieces when things went wrong and entertaining their friends. 'The uprightness of a child with a pure heart, standing here on earth beside me,' he said of her.

Purism

In 1917 Jeanneret was introduced by Auguste Perret to the painter Amédée Ozenfant, whose friendship helped him to emerge from his state of uncertainty and the contradictions of business life versus creative impulse. 'When I feel confused I think of your calm, sensitive, straightforward determination. A vast chasm seems to separate our ages. I'm on the threshold of discovery, you are at the stage of achievement.'

He had always drawn and painted. Walking in the Swiss Jura or travelling abroad, he produced a continuous stream of watercolours and drawings. The influence of his teacher, Charles L'Eplattenier, now merged with the influence of the Impressionists, Matisse and Signac. Yet at the age of thirty he had yet to find his own artistic voice. His first painting, *The Mantelpiece*, painted in 1918, can be considered (in both subject and style) as an important step forward and as a manifesto.

Jeanneret always wished he had been a painter, and he slightly resented his success as an architect. His first painting, *The Mantelpiece*, has the discipline and equilibrium that are to be found in all his work. Two books are lying on a mantelpiece beside a white cube: 'First painting 1918.... If the truth were known, the Acropolis lurks behind the painting somewhere.'

The severity of the composition and the intensity of the light foreshadow the Purist painting and architecture of the 1920s. From now on Jeanneret never ceased his activity as a painter. When he was young his teacher had convinced him to take up architecture. For the rest of his life he tried to raise his achievement as a practising painter to the same level as that of his architecture, as his reputation grew and grew.

Amédée Ozenfant and Charles-Edouard Jeanneret had many ideas in common. Both admired order and harmony, expressed in stark geometrical forms and broad expanses of pure colour. Both emphasized the importance of the machine. Cubism, a principal influence, seemed to have distanced itself too much from contemporary concerns. Their ideas were published in 1918 in a joint work entitled *Après le cubisme*. To define their aesthetic they reverted to the name 'Purism', originally coined by Ozenfant. The word covers not only the formal aspect of art but also a moral dimension: simplicity and economy of means were its defining qualities.

Above: a Purist still-life (1921). Below, from left to right: Amédée Ozenfant, Albert Jeanneret and Charles-Edouard Jeanneret (c. 1918).

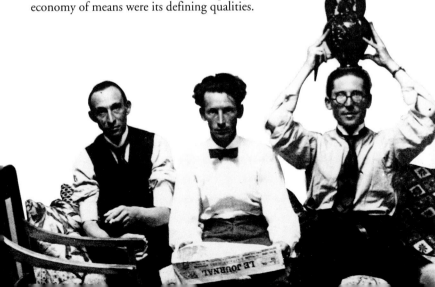

Jeanneret rehearsed the ideas and themes of Purism over and over again for nearly ten years, returning tirelessly in innumerable drawings and paintings to ordinary objects from daily life.

In order to achieve harmony and unity in his compositions he organized them according to what he called 'regulating lines'. He thought of a painting 'not as a surface but as a space', in which the objects are articulated in the same way as the built elements within an architectural space. Applied art, architecture and town planning are, in fact, 'manifestations of a single creative urge devoted to the various aspects of the visual phenomenon'.

Between 1918 and 1923, Jeanneret and Ozenfant exhibited their work together in a number of different galleries, before falling out in 1925. In 1920 Jeanneret had made the acquaintance of the painter Fernand Léger and they quickly became close friends; later they were to grow less close. Both men endowed technical progress and the machine with special importance in their art. Léger, however, included a social dimension in his outwardly 'machinist' works, whereas for Ozenfant and Jeanneret the values of Purism were essentially aesthetic and idealizing.

Until 1926 Jeanneret painted nothing but still lifes. Then he introduced some new, organic objects, 'objects provoking a poetic reaction': shells, bones, flints, pine-cones. Their more complex, sometimes distorted forms express a new lyrical feeling in his work. The gradual introduction of the female body, depicted with monumental and sculptural vigour, makes comparison with Léger and Picasso difficult to avoid.

At this stage Jeanneret achieved a new way of representing nature; henceforth strict order was the distinctive feature of his work in whatever medium

Fernand Léger's interest in architecture, the large size of his paintings and the increasing emphasis given in them to images of machinery explains his friendship with Le Corbusier. They talked frequently about the respective roles of the painter and the architect in the built environment and favoured close collaboration between artist and builder; this idea did not lead far, however. Above: a sketch of Léger by Le Corbusier.

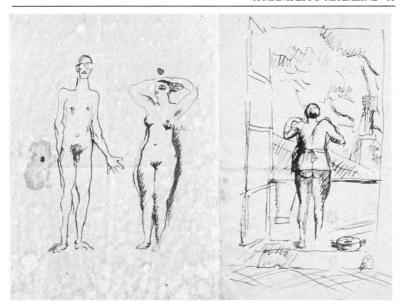

he chose. This long process represents a slow ripening of his art: 'Painting is a fearsome struggle, intense, relentless, private; a duel between the artist and himself. The struggle is interior, inside, unwitnessed from outside.'

The review *L'Esprit nouveau*

Amédée Ozenfant and Charles-Edouard Jeanneret became acquainted with the poet Paul Dermée and together they founded the review *L'Esprit nouveau*, apparently borrowing the title from a lecture given by the poet and novelist Guillaume Apollinaire in 1917, 'L'Esprit nouveau et les poètes'.

Twenty-eight issues of the review appeared between 1920 and 1925, before it finally failed. Adolf Loos, Elie Faure, Louis Aragon and Jean Cocteau were among the contributors. Ozenfant and Jeanneret wrote most of the articles, signing them with a variety of pseudonyms to give the impression that the magazine had many more contributors than it actually did! It was at this time that Jeanneret adopted the pseudonym Le Corbusier.

Le Corbusier was generally rather serious, a reflection perhaps of his upbringing and education. But his enjoyment of nature, his ideas about health and his love of the sea and swimming made him sympathetic to nudism, which he depicts here with gentle mockery. In the first sketch his large spectacles draw attention to his nakedness; in the second, Yvonne's apron does not quite manage to conceal all her charms.

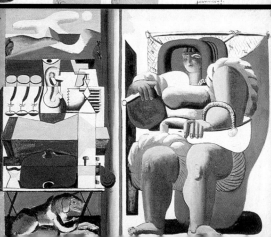

Throughout all his drawing, print-making, painting, tapestry, enamelling, architecture or town planning, Le Corbusier's aims and outlook remained the same: 'No one is just a sculptor, or just a painter or just an architect. Artistic creation of any kind is carried out in the service of poetry'. Painting was the 'secret laboratory' for his architecture and he spent a large part of his time doing it. After 1928 he abandoned Purism. Returning regularly to a few subjects – women, bulls, icons – he projected a new, less static and rationalistic vision, tending now towards something more elemental; here *Two Seated Women with Necklaces* (c. 1929), *Woman with Cat and Teapot* (1928) and *Fisherwoman, Arcachon* (1932). The colours are brighter, the contrasts more emphatic and the forms much more varied. He introduces natural objects alongside manufactured objects, but his painting nevertheless remains the work of an architect: the graphic style is powerful, planes and scale are juggled and the human body distorted and distended like monumental sculpture.

PAESTUM, *de 600 à 550 av. J.-C.*

Il faut tendre à l'établissement de *standarts* pour affronter le problème de la *perfection*.

Le Parthénon est un produit de sélection appliquée à un standart établi. Depuis déjà un siècle le temple grec était organisé dans tous ses éléments.

Lorsqu'un standart est établi, le jeu de la concurrence immédiate et violente s'exerce. C'est le match ; pour gagner, il faut faire mieux que l'adversaire *dans toutes les parties*, dans la ligne d'ensemble et dans tous les détails. C'est alors l'étude poussée des parties. Progrès.

Cliché de La Vie Automobile.   HUMBERT, 1907.

The aim of *L'Esprit nouveau*, 'the international review of aesthetics', was to point art and architecture in the direction of the contemporary industrial revolution. In matters of architecture the journal was more interested in function than in particular examples. It promoted the idea of 'standarts', responses to human need (in respect of form and organization) that are more or less universally applicable. It idealized the machine as a model of ingenuity and creativity, and juxtaposed (often provocatively) great works of architecture and modern industrial products. The journal championed the idea that architectural and industrial creation should be approached in the same way.

He used *L'Esprit nouveau* as a means of expression, a way of provoking people and a vehicle for developing his ideas. His methods of communication were extremely advanced for the period and included the use of arresting metaphors and interesting shock tactics. To proclaim the strength and beauty of a machine, a boat or an aeroplane he would pepper his text with photographs.

Vers une architecture

In 1923 Le Corbusier published *Vers une architecture*, a collection of a dozen articles that had appeared previously in *L'Esprit nouveau*; the book was to have a significant influence on the course of modern architecture. It was translated into several languages, including English under the title *Towards a New Architecture* in 1927, and helped to make the architect famous.

His basic doctrine is contained in it: that a new age has begun, with new social, economic and technical conditions to which the architect must respond, just as industry has responded. He emphasises that, when architecture is perceived in terms of masses and surfaces, 'the plan generates the whole', the architect needs to return to primary forms, as beautiful and comprehensible as possible,

Le Corbusier's book *Vers une architecture* won instant acclaim. The author demonstrated a talent for communication that was most unusual at the period amongst architects and planners. Le Corbusier designed the layout himself, as he did for most of his books. In spite of

increasing the accuracy of his plan by using a system of 'regulating lines – a guarantee against wilfulness'. In conclusion, he lays particular emphasis on the specificity of architecture in relation to construction: if industrial techniques are to be used in construction, permitting the production of 'mass-production houses', the architect's role – which has been drastically undermined by steel and concrete – should not stop at the mastery of techniques but should use 'the raw materials available to create striking, exciting relationships'.

far-reaching changes in architectural practices today, the book still commands a loyal readership and retains its power of persuasion.

A creative principle

The research done by Le Corbusier fuelled his preparations for real projects, which in turn, by allowing experiments to materialize, advanced the progress of subsequent theoretical investigations. Le Corbusier's large corpus of written work enriched this interaction between theory and practice, and between research and its applications.

Although he built a number of villas for the well-to-do between 1920 and 1930, Le Corbusier's primary aim was to fulfil the perceived social function of the architect, providing shelter and building cities. 'My own duty and my aim is to try and raise people out of their misery, away from catastrophe; to provide them with happiness, with a contented existence, with harmony. My own goal is to establish or re-establish harmony between people and their environment.'

Apartment blocks

In 1920 Le Corbusier drew up plans for the first example of low-cost housing – the Citrohan house – based on an

In the project for an 'immeuble villas' block (1922, above), Le Corbusier aimed to reconcile the needs of individuals with the needs of communal living. There were 120 'superimposed villas', offering a high degree of comfort (double-height living room and private garden terrace) plus the advantages of communal services. Below: the Citrohan house, the base unit of the 'immeuble villas'.

extremely simplified and rationalized design that would allow it to be mass-produced. At the Salon d'Automne in 1922 he presented his plan for a block of 'immeuble villas' (luxury flats) in which he sought to combine private living areas with communal areas in a building designed to

house one hundred families. This project was partly an expression of the scorn he felt for the outer suburbs of Paris, with their little private cottage-style dwellings; there were no communal services in these areas, space was squandered and commuting distances to Paris were long. The luxury flats were based on the observations made by the young Jeanneret in Italy in 1907 when he first visited the Carthusian monastery of Ema.

He was obsessed by the idea that 'the city must ensure individual liberty on a spiritual as well as a material level, and must endorse collective action as well'. Twenty years later this idea was the basis of his principle of the *Unité d'habitation*.

The *Esprit nouveau* pavilion at the Exposition Internationale in Paris (1925) was both a manifesto and a demonstration of architecture. The residential half consisted of the L-shaped design of one of the 'immeuble villas', surrounding an interior garden. Going against the 'decorative arts' style, Le Corbusier added furniture that could be bought in the shops – made of bentwood and metal. Storage space was provided by simple painted wooden modules. There were paintings and sculpture by Le Corbusier, Juan Gris, Fernand Léger, Amédée Ozenfant and Jacques Lipchitz. In the half of the pavilion dedicated to town planning, Le Corbusier and Pierre Jeanneret provided a vast diorama of townscape designs. The pavilion was demolished as soon as the exhibition was over; a replica was constructed in Bologna in 1977.

The *Esprit nouveau* pavilion

In 1925 the Exposition Internationale des Arts Décoratifs was held in Paris on the Esplanade des Invalides, Pont Alexandre III and around the Grand and the Petit Palais. It signalled architecture's final break with the decorative arts and Art Nouveau. Several revolutionary architects were given the opportunity to present their work. Robert Mallet-Stevens was responsible for the Tourism pavilion and the French pavilion, Tony Garnier for the pavilion of the city of Lyons. Le Corbusier designed the *Esprit nouveau* pavilion as a manifesto of his ideas on art and architecture. One side of the pavilion consisted of a dwelling similar in style to those in the 'immeuble villas' project; the other side, the extension to the living quarters, contained an

Le Corbusier's urban studies, whether they were idealized like his 'plan for a contemporary city of three million inhabitants' (below) or the Voisin plan, or more realistic like the 1937 plan (left) and the many studies he made that were more limited in scope, were never implemented.

The same was true of plans drawn up for other towns in Europe, Africa and America. The only exception was Chandigarh in India. The ambitious scope of the plans, their visionary nature and the provocative way they were presented made them non-viable in the eyes of the authorities. Their credibility was also compromised by their over-formal presentation and no accompanying studies to consider the technical, economic and legal factors.

exhibition of town-planning projects by Le Corbusier and Pierre Jeanneret.

The large town-planning projects

Le Corbusier continued with his theoretical work on town and city planning, his studies of traffic and density and his building and design projects. In 1922 he had unveiled a 'plan for a contemporary city of three million inhabitants' at the Salon d'Automne; it was presented as a diorama one hundred square metres (over one thousand square feet). Using theoretical terms, the architect aimed to draw attention to the acute planning problems afflicting Paris. He made

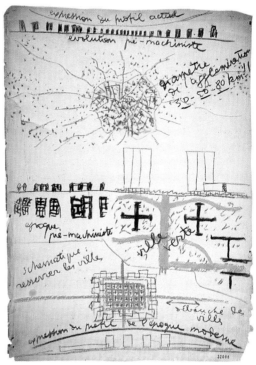

'four brutal axioms: 1. town centres must be made less congested; 2. town centres must be more densely built up; 3. means of transport must be increased; 4. there must be an increase in open spaces.'

The 'plan for a contemporary city of three million inhabitants' is a theoretical work, as is this sketch made during a lecture (above). Their principles, however – the reorganization of the different functions of the city, traffic management and the clearing of areas for parks and sports grounds – had an important influence on contemporary town planners.

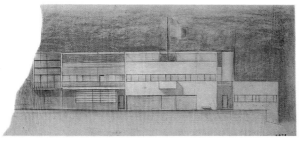

While this plan was not designed specifically with Paris in mind, his second great urban modernization project, the Voisin plan, which appeared in 1925, was. It was named after Gabriel Voisin, the manufacturer of cars and aeroplanes, who gave financial support to Le Corbusier, and was based on a circular scheme of ringed and radial streets. After 1930, in his studies of the 'Ville radieuse', Le Corbusier abandoned a concentric plan for the 'contemporary city' in favour of a linear organization. Different zones for different functions were still emphasized but the sectors were no longer enclosed one within another. Instead they stretched along the large arteries; these were divided into two categories corresponding to two different speed limits. This was the early stage of the development that culminated in the '7v' system applied at Chandigarh.

As a plan for Paris, however, the Voisin plan was unrealistic, calling for much of the old core of the city to be gutted. The 1937 plan for Paris presented a more pragmatic approach, though it still recommended sweeping changes in the capital, including a central business area surrounded by a network of motorways radiating out towards the regions of France.

Purist villas

Although now considering himself primarily a designer of cities and the inventor of a new type of low-cost housing, Le Corbusier continued to devote a large proportion of his time between 1920 and 1930 to the design and construction of private houses for a clientèle that was receptive to contemporary art and modern architecture. Out of about twenty designs, sixteen villas

were built and most of them are still in a good state of repair today. The architect's clients were generally members of wealthy families. Some of them – Lipchitz, Ozenfant, Miestchaninoff, Ternisien and Planeix – were artists, whilst others – Cook, La Roche and Stein – were collectors. Most of the villas were built to the west of Paris, either on the edge of the city or in the suburbs: Auteuil, Boulogne, La Celle-Saint-Cloud, Garches, Poissy.

These villas vary greatly in layout, often because of problems posed by their site – very small plots of land, neighbourhood constraints – but they express their architect's key ideas very forcefully. Several of them show clear evidence of the principles developed in the Citrohan house and the 'immeuble villa' blocks. The organization of interior spaces is very carefully considered, as is the relationship between vertical and horizontal movement, sometimes linked by a sloping ramp.

Thanks to 'reinforced concrete which obviates the need for walls' and to post-and-beam construction, Le Corbusier liberates space, opening out one area into another, accentuating the sense of being able to see through the dwelling from one end to the other and admitting the maximum amount of sunlight – plus a view of trees. The living room is often of double

The Villa Stein-de-Monzie in Garches (left and above) was built for two separate families in 1928. Although it is double, its layout is extremely straightforward and illustrates the architect's search for consistency and uniformity. The outside walls reflect the interior organization precisely. Openings – loggias and bow-windows – conform to strict rules, imposed by the system (relied on increasingly by Le Corbusier) of *tracés régulateurs* (regulating lines). Long windows predominate. The roof and verticals make a framework for the whole. The walls are smooth and blank. The architect used the same principles in the Villa Church in Ville-d'Avray (opposite above), also built in 1928.

height. The open layout encourages an 'architectural stroll' and a fluid reading of the architecture as it 'comes and goes'. Two villas are of particular interest: the double Villa La Roche-Jeanneret and the Villa Savoye; both exemplify aspects of Le Corbusier's thinking at the end of the 1920s.

The Villa La Roche-Jeanneret

The Villa La Roche-Jeanneret, in Auteuil in Paris, was built in 1925 at the far end of a cul-de-sac bordered on either side by small houses and gardens. It was designed for two families. The two dwellings are housed in a single block and the outside gives no clue as to where they divide.

La Roche was a banker, a bachelor and a collector of Cubist and Purist paintings; he had asked Le Corbusier to design a villa in which he could display his collection. The requirements of the Jeanneret family, consisting of Le Corbusier's brother Albert, his wife, Lotti Raaf, and her two daughters, were very different. The layout of their villa was of necessity much more traditional than that of the banker's home; the normal arrangement in fact is reversed in this villa, the bedrooms being on the

At the Villa La Roche-Jeanneret Le Corbusier gave pride of place to the picture gallery, a curved area raised above ground level. A gently sloping ramp occupies one of the long walls of the gallery, joining the upper to the ground floor. The main entrance hall is two storeys high. Three of the four sides of the hall have either a gangway or a gallery, giving a variety of views of the paintings, an 'architectural promenade' for the feet and the eyes. Opposite: more intimate in scale, the living room of Albert Jeanneret's villa.

ground floor and the dining and sitting rooms upstairs; the main rooms have access to the roof terrace.

The Villa Savoye

The Villa Savoye was built on a spacious site at Poissy in 1931, for the family of an insurance broker. The rectangular prism in concrete is something of an architectural manifesto on Le Corbusier's part. Perched on narrow *pilotis* (supporting columns) and arranged on a geometrical grid, the house is 'a box in the air, pierced all round by a horizontal window'. Damaged during the war and threatened with demolition twenty years later to make way for a school, the Villa Savoye was saved at the last minute after an international petition; it was listed by André Malraux in 1964 as a historic monument, when Le Corbusier was still alive.

To work is to breathe

Architect, town planner, painter and writer, Le Corbusier was capable of exceptional hard work; this was not only due to the solid habits of study he had

Overleaf: the Villa Savoye in Poissy, called 'Les Heures claires', contains all of Le Corbusier's vocabulary, expressed with such concentrated power and intensity as to transcend the 'five points of the new architecture' (written in 1925, but published in 1927). The main rooms open on to an interior garden. A ramp leads to a roof-terrace/solarium protected from the wind by screen walls. The 'architectural promenade' is to be enjoyed here in its fullest sense.

SAVOYE

SAVOYE

acquired as a boy in his native Jura, but also to his great organizational abilities and his very strong streak of ambition. 'Work is not a punishment, to work is to breathe! And breathing is an extremely regular bodily function: never too heavy, never too light, but continuous.' He was also driven by a need to create: 'The supreme joy, the only real joy, is creation'.

He continued to expand his circle of acquaintances, to exhibit, to travel, to make lecture tours in Europe and North and South America. Although he steadfastly refused to teach, he enjoyed airing his ideas in public, illustrating his lectures with diagrams prepared in advance on large sheets of white paper or sketches made as he was speaking. After his first visit to the Soviet Union in 1928 he went on a lecture tour in 1929 to Buenos Aires and Rio de Janeiro.

In 1935 he made his first trip to the USA, where, on his arrival by boat in New York, he stunned journalists by immediately declaring that the skyscrapers of Manhattan were too small. His remark was not meant as a pleasantry or a provocation, but simply expressed his opinion about the business centres of modern cities: they should be densely built up, with very high tower blocks, in order to provide more space for parks and gardens at ground level. He expressed this opinion in a book written about the United States in 1937: *Quand les cathédrales étaient blanches*, which was published in English in 1947 as *When the Cathedrals were White*.

For Le Corbusier concrete was as natural as stone. He had a highly developed feel for materials, looking for density, grain, roughness or smoothness. He was often still designing his buildings while they were under construction, correcting and perfecting details, working out items not in the first draft, dispelling his own anxieties. He enjoyed being with the workmen on the site. In his book *Vers une architecture* he sings the praises of engineers. 'Engineers are manly and fit, busy and useful, upright and joyful', whereas 'architects are cynical and idle, either boastful or morose'. If architecture is designed to provoke an emotional reaction, and construction simply needs to 'stay up', he looks forward to a profession that will combine engineering and architecture (the right and left hands of the art of building) in a permanent and amicable dialogue. Above: *Two Men on a Building Site* and *The Engineer and the Architect*.

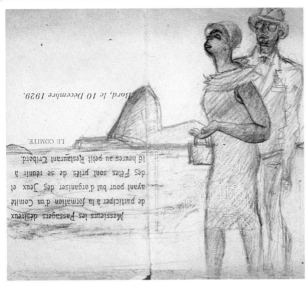

Bord, le 10 Décembre 1929.

LE COMITÉ.

16 heures au petit Restaurant Cribord.

des Fêtes sont priés de se réunir à

ayant pour but d'organiser des Jeux et

de participer à la formation d'un Comité

Messieurs les Passagers désireux

In 1929 Le Corbusier made his first visit to South America. On the steamer *Giulio Cesare* he made the acquaintance of Josephine Baker, who had taken Paris by storm four years earlier in *La Revue nègre*. He named the singer 'pure-hearted Josephine' and produced several touching drawings and portraits of her.

Henry Frugès, a Bordeaux industrialist who made a fortune in sugar, discovered Le Corbusier in 1923 when he read his book *Vers une architecture*. He first asked him to build him a house in Bordeaux, and then to build two groups of workers' housing: seven houses at Lège and fifty-three at Pessac. Below: the model of a house at Pessac.

Lège and Pessac: two housing projects

In 1923 the industrialist Henry Frugès, owner of a sugar refinery near Bordeaux, an amateur painter and passionate admirer of modern art, commissioned Le Corbusier to design two groups of dwellings for his workers, one at Lège, the other at Pessac. This commission gave the architect the opportunity to put his theories about social housing and the planned environment into practice. At Pessac he built fifty-three dwellings; the houses were either semi-detached or joined in terraces, and all were built on the same basic module. Le Corbusier tried out his theory of exterior polychromy at Pessac, attempting with the interplay of whites, blues, greens and browns on façades and gable-ends to co-ordinate and to enliven the ensemble.

In spite of technical difficulties with the concrete, and serious financial problems, Henry Frugès supported his architect with exceptional loyalty.

Corseaux, a small house

From 1924 to 1925 Le Corbusier built La Petite Maison for his parents, at Corseaux, near Vevey, on the shores of Lake Geneva; it is a model of minimalist architecture – in size as well as in materials. Le Corbusier's father died in 1926 and only lived in La Petite Maison for a year. His mother, 'a woman of faith and courage', 'surrounded by the affectionate admiration of her family', lived there until her death in 1960 in her hundred and first year.

Using a five-metre (sixteen-foot) square as his basic module, Le Corbusier (opposite) built four different types of house at Pessac, joining them together in a variety of different arrangements. Construction work was disastrously hampered by technical and financial problems. The development then suffered disfigurement at the hands of the owner/occupiers, but is now undergoing restoration.

Two palaces: two setbacks

Neither of two large projects, the Palace of the League of Nations in Geneva, entered for a competition in 1927, and the Palace of the Soviets in Moscow, for which he presented a design in 1931, was built.

The jury for the League of Nations building, having originally short-listed the Le Corbusier-Jeanneret design with eight others (out of 377 entries), then disqualified the project on the grounds that the entry consisted of reproductions of the plans and not the originals.

Below left: front view of La Petite Maison at Corseaux. 'The lake is 4 metres from the window.... There is 300 square metres of floor to keep clean, in return for which an incomparably fine, uninterrupted view can be enjoyed.... The house is 2½ metres high, and is the shape of a long box. The dawn can be greeted at one end through an oblique skylight, and the sun is in front of the house for the rest of the day. The local council of a nearby hamlet has met to discuss the "crime against nature" perpetrated by such architecture, and, terrified that it might be copied at some time (who knows?), have prohibited such imitations in perpetuity.'
Le Corbusier, 1954

A conspiracy on the part of some diplomats with no taste for contemporary architecture and some architects who cared more for convention than creation thus overturned an imaginative scheme that was carefully worked out in every detail: perfectly fitted to the site, efficient, accessible, with good acoustics....

Le Corbusier was mortified by his first important defeat and expressed his bitterness in writing several times. In 1928 he published *Une maison, un palais* and, in a preface to the third edition of *Vers une architecture*, he voiced his indignation once again: 'We submitted a modern palace to Geneva. Phew, what a scandal!... Polite society expects a palace, and for them a real palace is like the one they saw on their honeymoon, in a land of princes and cardinals, doges and kings.'

The plan for the Palace of the Soviets was prepared for a competition held by the Soviet authorities; it was to be erected quite near the Kremlin. The dominant features of the plan entered by Le Corbusier and Pierre Jeanneret were two vast auditoria, one seating 15,000 and the other 6500, to be constructed at either end of a monumental building.

The model of the Palace of the Soviets (below) shows a spacious group of buildings developed along a central axis with a large auditorium at either end. The roof of the larger auditorium is supported by a majestic arch.

In 1923 the city of Geneva offered the League of Nations a site for their new headquarters. An international competition was launched and the League decided to appoint a jury of nine architects. Le Corbusier saw this competition as a means of gaining international recognition. His entry (left) comprises elements from classical monumental architecture couched in a thoroughly modern ensemble, containing a number of features typical of his style: free plan, *pilotis*, horizontal windows, terraces. The scheme was rejected, however, and a group of architects from different countries was appointed to carry out the design at the request of a committee of five diplomats who had been selected by the jury.

The Soviet authorities were alarmed by the modernity of the project, and *Pravda* commented, in January 1932, on the 'spirit of naked "industrialism", dubious here because it is handled as if it were a sort of congress-hangar'. Le Corbusier, who had the support of several friends in this international venture, tried to make contact with the Soviet authorities and suggested a compromise with Zoltovsky, the winning architect, but he was no more successful than he had been in Geneva.

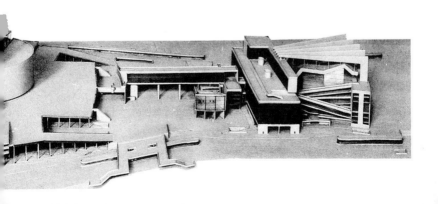

Paris, Geneva, Moscow: projects completed

Between 1928 and 1930 Le Corbusier and Pierre Jeanneret were responsible for a number of sizeable projects. The Centrosoyus (central statistical office) in Moscow followed a double international competition; it is an imposing group, combining buildings with curved and prismatic shapes.

The Salvation Army's hostel (Cité de Refuge) in eastern Paris is built on a very small site and comprises three different service areas: restaurants, hostels for men and women and workshops. Initially, the façade of the main building consisted of a vast, closed expanse of glass, double-glazed – the 'neutralizing wall' – the ventilation inside to be provided in summer and winter by an air-conditioning system designed to deliver air at the right temperature. Technical and financial problems swiftly led to it being abandoned.

The Pavillon Suisse, a hostel for Swiss students in the Cité Universitaire in Paris, contains forty-seven rooms and various service premises. Some aspects of the layout foreshadow the principles used later in the *Unités d'habitation*.

In 1929 the Salvation Army began planning a new hostel (left) in Paris to house five hundred homeless people. The Princesse de Polignac financed the project and chose Le Corbusier as its architect. The complex requirements of the building gave him the opportunity to try out his theories on social housing. He made a framework of reinforced concrete floors and columns, a brick façade (facing north) and a glass façade (facing south), consisting of a steel structure covered in a solid sheet of glass measuring nearly 1000 square metres [over 1000 square feet]. The air-conditioning that was supposed to control the temperature of the glass façade proved unequal to the task and the glass had to be replaced with windows that opened and closed, behind multi-coloured sun-screens. Access to the building was via a portico and a gangway (borrowed from the design of passenger ships), and there was also a small circular entrance of glass bricks made by the Saint-Gobain factory in 1928. The use of inexpensive and plain materials, such as metal, glass and tiles, expressed both the taste of Le Corbusier and the principles of the Salvation Army.

The Molitor block of flats is near the Bois de Boulogne, between Paris and the suburb of Boulogne-sur-Seine. The basic structure is reinforced concrete but the façade is entirely glazed and articulated by projecting bays. Above the sixth floor on the roof terrace Le Corbusier built the studio apartment he was to inhabit from 1934 until his death in 1965. The studio faces east; when not travelling, Le Corbusier spent every morning painting, reserving architecture and office work for the afternoon.

The Clarté flats were commissioned by Edmond Wanner, a manufacturer specializing in metal building materials, to be built in south-eastern Geneva. They were experimental in several respects: in a large number of the flats the living area was double height, metallic structural elements, including door and window frames, were to a great extent standardized and prefabricated, and glass was widely used.

Here Le Corbusier revived the use of glass tiles on the staircases, first employed by the American architect

A double row of *pilotis* buried deep into the ground (which is riddled with old quarries) supports the concrete floor carrying the framework of the main building of the Pavillon Suisse at the Cité Universitaire in Paris. The structural elements were pre-cast in a factory; the interior walls are not attached to the framework and this gives excellent sound-proofing to the forty-seven rooms. The entrance and reception area are in a small adjoining building. The stairwell is lit by a wall made of glass bricks.

R. H. Turnock in his eight-storey Brewster building, constructed in Chicago in 1890.

The Weissenhof and the 'five points of the new architecture'

In 1927 the Deutscher Werkbund, which had been founded in 1907 to encourage the integration of art, industry and craft, announced its plan to build housing (houses and flats) on the Weissenhof, a hill near Stuttgart. The buildings were designed by some of the most innovatory architects of the day. Mies van der Rohe, vice-president of the Werkbund, was put in charge of the project. The fifteen or so artists involved, besides Mies himself, included Peter Behrens, J. J. P. Oud, Bruno and Max Taut, Ludwig Hilberseimer, Walter Gropius, Victor Bourgeois, Adolf Rading and Josef Frank. Le Corbusier designed two private houses at the Weissenhof, based on the same principles as the Citrohan house. The site constituted a unique architectural experiment; the juxtaposition of so many plans and ideas provoked heated debate in artistic and architectural circles.

The Molitor block of flats, built on the border of Paris and the suburb of Boulogne-sur-Seine, enjoys an unimpeded view over the city. The façade is a transparent curtain wall: a fine metal framework painted and partly overhanging holds the window panes and the Nevada glass bricks. Le Corbusier built his own apartment-cum-studio on the roof terrace, with a barrel-vaulted roof.

The *pilotis* of the Pavillon Suisse in the Cité Universitaire lift the building four metres (thirteen feet) into the air, freeing the ground floorspace and emphasizing the contrast between the park and the 'built box'.

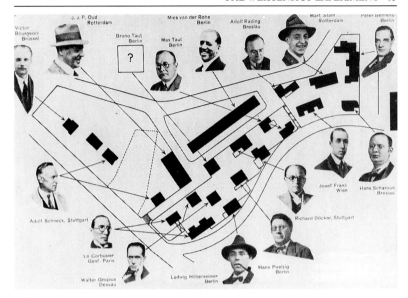

Le Corbusier's manifesto on the 'five points of the new architecture', published as the Weissenhof was being built, was bound to lend fuel to the debate. He presented the conclusions reached over the years from the study of his projects, on the importance of reinforced concrete to the key elements of modern architecture; his analysis was deliberately schematic: 1. *pilotis* 2. free plan 3. horizontal windows 4. free façade 5. roof terrace. Each point can be considered separately, but all are connected. The formulation of the five points, simple and almost dogmatic, is uncharacteristic of Le Corbusier's usually pragmatic and open approach to every new project. It might also seem to diminish the richness and diversity of the work itself. Nevertheless, the 'five points' sum up the principles underlying most of his constructions as far as the relationship between structure and form is concerned, and the opportunities offered to both by reinforced concrete.

The first buildings to contain elements of the 'five points' were over thirty years old. In 1889 William Le Baron Jenney had built the Leiter Building in Chicago,

At the Weissenhof Le Corbusier built two houses side by side that illustrate his 'five points of the new architecture' very clearly. He wanted to introduce as much standardization and industrialization as possible into his buildings, and to demonstrate the advantages of low-cost mass production. He also hoped to show that building with standardized elements could create a fresh aesthetic and offer great freedom to architects, who could combine the elements in a huge variety of ways.

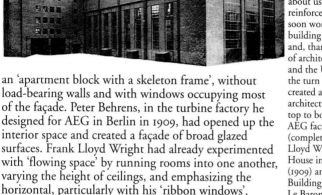

Although architects were diffident about using it at first, reinforced concrete soon won a place in building programmes and, thanks to a handful of architects in Europe and the United States at the turn of the century, created a revolution in architecture. Left, from top to bottom: Behrens' AEG factory in Berlin (completed 1909), Frank Lloyd Wright's Robie House in Chicago (1909) and the Leiter Building by William Le Baron Jenney (completed 1892), also in Chicago. The logic of a building's use and its appearance are

an 'apartment block with a skeleton frame', without load-bearing walls and with windows occupying most of the façade. Peter Behrens, in the turbine factory he designed for AEG in Berlin in 1909, had opened up the interior space and created a façade of broad glazed surfaces. Frank Lloyd Wright had already experimented with 'flowing space' by running rooms into one another, varying the height of ceilings, and emphasizing the horizontal, particularly with his 'ribbon windows'.

When Walter Gropius designed the Fagus shoe-tree factory at Alfeld an der Leine in 1911, and the Bauhaus buildings at Dessau in 1926, neither used load-bearing

reconciled; construction and architecture, both now respond appropriately to their distinct roles, thanks to the framework of columns and beams or columns and floors. In formulating his 'five points', Le Corbusier wanted to clarify the current position and pave the way for future developments. His genius lay not so much in drawing up the five points as in the combined implementation of them and the clarity with which he formulated them.

walls; the façades are glazed, with no supports at the corners, and are detached from the structural frame inside the building. The De Stijl group, founded in Holland by Theo van Doesburg in 1917, developed its own ideas on the unity of house design and the interpenetration of vertical and horizontal surfaces. The Schröder house, designed by Gerrit Rietveld in Utrecht in 1924, successfully embodies the ideas of the De Stijl group. Mies van der Rohe exploited all the structural potential of reinforced concrete in order to free the interior space, to maximize intercommunication, both within the house and between the interior and the exterior, and to achieve transparency, the latter particularly in his plan for a transparent skyscraper (1919–21) and, in 1923, his country houses. His contribution to the Weissenhof was a block of flats built on a steel frame that allowed a true free-plan layout.

'Equipment for living'

It was Le Corbusier's contention that every aspect of a dwelling should be a concern of the architect, including the region and town where it was to be built, the house itself and its interior decoration. His taste in furniture

The independent framework of a reinforced concrete house consists of beams and floors supported by columns, allowing walls to be omitted so that the interior space can be arranged and divided as required. This 'free plan' means that spaces can run together and each storey can be organized differently. In addition, because the framework is independent, the façade can be a free-standing glass curtain wall. The structure and insulation are also separate. The roof terrace/garden gives access to sun, air and light. Above: the open-plan hall in the Villa Stein-de Monzie, Garches.

became simpler and simpler, with the aim of returning furniture to its essential functions. A table, chair, armchair, chaise longue and a bed had to respond to biological needs and to be designed to fit the human body. Books, household utensils and linen could be stored in simple, all-purpose units. He spoke not of furniture but of 'equipment for living'.

In his Purist villas he encouraged his clients to choose ordinary furniture, designed by no one in particular. He particularly favoured Thonet bentwood chairs. He began designing objects himself, according to the strictest principles: they had to meet certain functional norms, to be suited to the architecture and to be capable of being mass-produced. He created storage units that could be incorporated into the architecture, side by side and one on top of the other.

Between 1926 and 1930 various architects and designers experimented with furniture made on a framework of steel tubing. Eileen Gray created her adjustable table and Marcel Breuer his famous Wassily armchair. In 1927 Mies van der Rohe and Mart Starm presented their steel frame furniture at the Weissenhof. In 1928, in collaboration with Pierre Jeanneret and the furniture designer Charlotte Perriand, who had joined the office in Rue de Sèvres in 1927, Le Corbusier presented a whole range of furniture that the partnership then used in the Villa Church and the Villa La Roche. The furniture and the storage units were exhibited at the Salon d'Automne in Paris in 1929. The furniture makes a strong impact because structurally it is pared down to bare essentials, and its simple structures fit well with the other

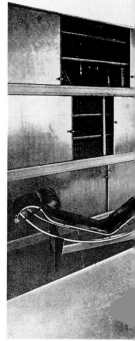

Le Corbusier persuaded Charlotte Perriand (above) to move away from the decorative arts tradition in interior design. She worked with him and Pierre Jeanneret from 1927 to 1937, and again in the 1950s.

architectural elements; originally produced by
Thonet, the various designs have gradually become
modern classics.

L'Art décoratif d'aujourd'hui

In 1925 Le Corbusier published *L'Art décoratif
d'aujourd'hui* in which he voiced his opinions on the
subject usually known as 'decoration'. His illustrations
were designed to surprise, at least, if not to shock: the
chapter on museums opens with a picture of a bidet.
Aeroplane fuselages, electric turbines and Voisin cars
are juxtaposed with Louis XV chests-of-drawers. The
message is bitingly clear: the objects that surround us are
our servants; they must be appropriate and unobtrusive.
Le Corbusier denounces the reverence in which the
past is held and rejects the notion that we should find
models in museums. In his view, folklore is useful only

Le Corbusier reduced
furnishings to basic
essentials, 'equipment
for living', the aesthetic
and moral equivalent
of the Purist architecture
of his villas, which he
sometimes furnished
himself (above, the
library of Villa Church).
Armchairs, tables and
shelving are simple
structures, designed
with an extreme
economy of line and
using simple materials.

if it helps us understand the laws of creation and function. He promulgates the provocative 'Ripolin law' (Ripolin being the trade name of a brand of paint): 'Every citizen should replace his wallpapers, wall-hangings, stencils with a coat of white Ripolin. Cleanse your home…then cleanse yourself.…'

The lesson of the book is brief and to the point: 'Modern decorative art is not decorated'. The perfection of an object, for Le Corbusier, is generated by the technical and economic constraints attendant on its design and construction. Although he rejected a functionalist concept of architecture, because architecture 'is above and beyond utilitarian matters', he appeared to support functionalism for objects made by industrial processes.

The CIAM (Congrès Internationaux d'Architecture Moderne)

In 1928 and for the next thirty years or so, Le Corbusier found an international forum for the exchange of ideas and information that he deemed so necessary. In that year, with some friends, and with generous financial support from Hélène de Mandrot, he held a preliminary gathering of architects, artists, art critics and politicians whose aim was to consider, in depth and across national boundaries, various aspects of architecture and town planning.

This initiative gave birth to the regular international conferences on modern architecture known as the CIAM. Each congress had a specific theme: the foundations of modern architecture, the search for a new aesthetic, low-cost housing, housing clusters, town planning, housing and leisure, architecture and aesthetics, new towns and social centres, the inner city, the human habitat.

The 1933 Congress, one of the most productive, gave birth to *La Charte d'Athènes*, published in 1943, in which

Maison Pirsoul.

AUTRES ICONES LES MUSÉES

In *L'Art décoratif d'aujourd'hui* Le Corbusier juxtaposes necessary, practical objects with traditional pieces from museums.

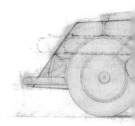

Le Corbusier set out his ideas on the main functions of the city – as a place in which one lived, cultivated one's mind and body, worked, moved about and preserved the national heritage.

Participants in the first CIAM in 1928: Le Corbusier is standing to the right of Hélène de Mandrot (in the middle) and Pierre Jeanneret, second from the left in the front row.

Le Corbusier took a keen interest in motorcars. In 1925 he bought a large Voisin and often photographed it in front of his buildings. In 1928 he began designing a 'minimum' (sometimes called 'maximum') car, returning to the project in 1936 (left).

The years that followed the Second World War were to witness the full flowering of Le Corbusier's talent. The *Unité d'habitation* in Marseilles embodied his ideas about social housing. The chapel at Ronchamp used concrete to give expression to an extraordinary loftiness of spirit. With his painting, sculpture, tapestry and print-making, Le Corbusier achieved a 'synthesis of all the arts'.

CHAPTER 4

FULL BLOOM

The *Unité d'habitation* (opposite) in Marseilles illustrates how far ahead of his contemporary artists and architects Le Corbusier was. In spite of obstacles, he spent five important years of his life supervising the construction of this project – the physical expression of his meditations on architecture and town planning.

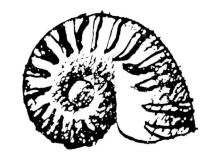

The outbreak of war and then the occupation of France by Germany put a stop to almost all building work. Le Corbusier drew up some plans for refugee encampments and prefabricated school buildings, some of them in collaboration with Jean Prouvé, but in June 1940 he decided to close his office.

With his wife and his cousin Pierre Jeanneret he took refuge for a few months in Ozon, a small village in the Pyrenees, where he spent his time writing and drawing. Some of the paintings and sculptures in his series called after the village, *Ozon*, produced some years later, developed from sketches made at this time.

Stalemate with the Vichy government

In 1941 Le Corbusier was appointed by the then minister for the interior, Marcel Peyrouton, to the government campaign against unemployment. Shortly afterwards he joined a committee set up to find ways of reinvigorating the building industry.

Throughout his career Le Corbusier made a consistent attempt to win the support of the authorities for his architectural and town-planning projects. More often than not his contacts with the world of politics came to grief. The novelty of his ideas, the

In 1924 Le Corbusier set up office in a former Jesuit monastery at 35 Rue de Sèvres in Paris. It consisted of a long room, with ten windows on one side only; the draughtsmen's desks are lined up opposite the windows. Le Corbusier first shared the running of the office with his cousin Pierre Jeanneret; later it was taken over by André Wogensky, until 1956. A constant stream of students and young architects passed through. They were eager to learn from the master and often gave their services free. Later they spread his ideas all over the world.

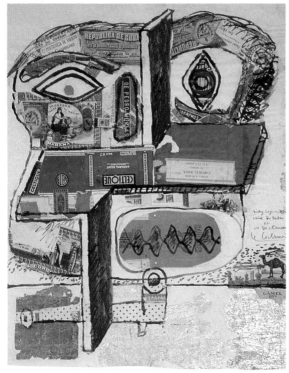

In 1928 Le Corbusier began experiments in his painting and sculpture that took him further and further from the cool severity of the work he had done earlier in the 1920s. He assembled bones, roots and ropes, 'objects provoking a poetic reaction'. He began including figures and juxtaposing lines, surfaces and colours with new vigour. Monumental female figures began to appear frequently. From 1939 to 1940 his *Ubu* and *Ozon* series reiterated what he called 'acoustic forms', which were sometimes based on themes from his Purist days; he repeated these in sculptures. The workings of the subconscious and a Surrealist dimension began to appear. In a collage created in Vichy during the war, *Tobacco Crisis and the Life of Camel* (left), at a time when food was short and tobacco rationed, he used different kinds of cigar and cigarette packets, including the Camel packet with its famous icon, to create this disquieting face, above the white pipe that is often a feature of his Purist paintings.

ambitious scope of his projects and the often dogmatic thrust of his rhetoric scared the authorities, who were in general unreceptive to the problems that modern architecture addressed.

Nor was he a master of diplomacy. Conservatives regarded him as a communist, socialists as a fascist. In fact, the wide range of his contacts suggests that he entertained no political bias at all in his approaches to the authorities.

His desire was simply to build and equip cities, and he addressed his requests to anyone who might offer him the wherewithal to do so. When he wrote *La Ville radieuse* in 1935 he dedicated it 'To Authority', and later mailed it personally to Stalin, Mussolini, Pétain and Nehru.

A decade of exceptional productivity

The gradual re-opening of his office after the war, after a break of nearly ten years, was a period of intense activity for Le Corbusier, in architecture and town planning as well as in the applied arts and in writing. A law passed on 31 December 1940 decreed that anyone with the title of architect had to be a member of the architects' professional association. Le Corbusier (and Auguste Perret) requested membership of the body, although they did not have the required academic qualifications; but their work was taken into account and Le Corbusier was made a member on 20 April 1944.

The large number of projects completed by Le Corbusier's office in the space of the next few years is impressive, and refutes the commonly held opinion that he theorized prolifically and produced little.

The *Unité d'habitation* in Marseilles

In 1945 the French government took steps to end the acute housing shortage with which it was faced after the war and to set up a public housing programme. Raoul Dautry, whose acquaintance Le Corbusier had made when he was

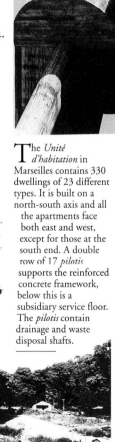

The *Unité d'habitation* in Marseilles contains 330 dwellings of 23 different types. It is built on a north-south axis and all the apartments face both east and west, except for those at the south end. A double row of 17 *pilotis* supports the reinforced concrete framework, below this is a subsidiary service floor. The *pilotis* contain drainage and waste disposal shafts.

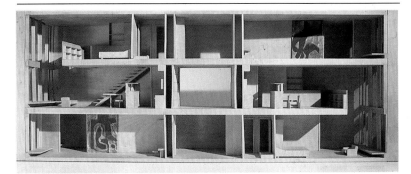

working for the railways, was the minister in charge of reconstruction and planning. He was an admirer of modern architecture and commissioned Le Corbusier to build a block of flats in Marseilles.

Le Corbusier welcomed this opportunity to put into practice the ideas he had been working on for the past twenty-five years. He saw the project as experimental in four ways: in the conception of the dwelling-places, in the building techniques, in the use of background social research and in the integration of the block with urban planning. Le Corbusier was averse to the garden cities that had been built on the outskirts of large towns and instead offered 'vertical garden cities' based on his earliest designs for 'immeuble villas' (1922). He wished to demonstrate how modern building techniques could satisfy individual and collective needs in the same building. The memory of the Carthusian monastery at Ema in Tuscany, which he had discovered in 1907, was still with him. He built the block of flats as an 'unité d'habitation de grandeur conforme' (to human proportions), thus named because the dimensions of the rooms and the layout of their fixtures and fittings were designed with reference to the dimensions of the human body.

Entrance to the apartments in the *Unités* is sometimes on the upper floor and sometimes on the lower and these are linked by interior staircases. Rooms are 3.66 metres wide and 2.26 metres high, or 4.84 metres in the double-height areas of the living room. The dimensions are based on Modulor (the framework is a module 4.19 metres square).

The *pilotis* raise the first floor of the *Unité* to 8 metres (26 feet) high, leaving the ground free. The roof terrace is also usable space and for Le Corbusier this was an important element in the social function of the communal apartment block. Interior 'streets' on the 7th and 8th floors house shops and the roof terrace has a nursery school, a gymnasium, a running track, a small tiered theatre and 'artificial hills' for young children. This was not created solely to satisfy the material needs of the inhabitants: for Le Corbusier the space between the sky and the city represented the Mediterranean. He composed the children's terrace, playing with solids and voids, harmonizing curved and straight lines, orchestrating a grand fresco in concrete. The canopy over the gymnasium, the ventilation and lift shafts, the walls of the solarium, the flights of stairs, the seats against the safety parapets constitute a colossal 'acoustic sculpture', a work whose shapes interact and catch the eye, leading one's gaze outwards to the vast view beyond the building – both transmitting and receiving impressions 'acoustically'.

The *Unité d'habitation* in Marseilles was both a working model and an experiment with new techniques. The plumbing, waste disposal and air conditioning were all innovatory. More unusual still was the degree of comfort in the individual dwellings. They were forty-five per cent larger than the permitted minimum size and the sound-proofing had never been so effective in any previous public housing scheme. In spite of all the problems and all the adverse criticism, local authorities and architects learnt many important lessons. Three other *Unités d'habitation* were built: Nantes-Rezé (1953–5, above left), Briey, near Metz (1955–8) and Firminy, near Saint-Etienne (1965–7). Le Corbusier also produced plans for a *Unité* in Berlin (1956–8) but he did not build it himself.

The building was designed for communal ownership. It has a structural framework of reinforced concrete; the floors, ceilings and walls of the apartments are independent of this framework and the soundproofing is therefore perfect. The apartments are connected by seven interior 'streets', one of them lined with shops and a hotel. The north side of the block is windowless; on the other three sides are balconies belonging to the apartments. Although the apartments are deep, they are well-lit and the lighting is carefully controlled. The plumbing system is meticulously planned. Each apartment is air-conditioned. The interiors, designed with Charlotte Perriand, are unusually well-organized and equipped, and include all manner of built-in storage space. A little hatch permits deliveries to be made directly from the 'street' into the kitchen.

The prefabrication of the various elements presented problems and these and other technical difficulties caused massive delays in construction. The state found it difficult to come to terms with the originality of Le Corbusier's project, and a number of the architect's most determined opponents did their best to undermine the scheme.

Work on it was stopped several times, and eventually took five years to complete; in the unstable political climate of the postwar Fourth Republic, six ministers of reconstruction and planning came and went. Begun in October 1947, the 'Fada' block, as the inhabitants of Marseilles called it, was officially inaugurated on 14 October 1952.

In social terms the *Unité d'habitation* did not fulfil the expectations of its creator. Almost immediately after its inauguration the state began selling off apartments so that, by 1954, the block was in multiple ownership in the usual way. The common services stopped functioning or functioned badly; the shops in the interior street, virtually inaccessible from outside, found it difficult to keep going; the gym on the roof terrace was soon privatized. However, from the point of view of innovation in habitat design, building techniques and town planning the project marked a crucial step forward and was an unquestionable success.

André Wogenscky was in charge of building works for the *Unité d'habitation* in Marseilles and soon began to take a particular interest in the equipment of the individual apartments. Labour-saving devices were just beginning to appear in the 1950s. Wogenscky appreciated the progress being made but disliked the disorderly way in which the various units were arranged. Charlotte Perriand, who had not worked for Le Corbusier since 1937, now joined the team in charge of the *Unité* and made an important contribution to the design of the interiors. Kitchens were installed with an unusual amount of built-in equipment – ventilation fans, waste disposal units, refrigerators, electric cookers.

Ronchamp, poetry in concrete

In the years following the Second World War, through the impetus of two priests, Pères Couturier and Régamey, the French government commissioned a programme of religious art and church building, designed to foster artistic and architectural skills.

The churches built in this way were all remarkable works of modernism. The one begun on the Plateau d'Assy in 1937 and finished in 1957 had interior decorations by the painters Bazaine, Chagall, Léger, Lurçat and Rouault; its architect, Maurice Novarina, also designed the new church at Audincourt in 1949, with interior decoration by Bazaine, Léger and Le Moal. From 1947 to 1951 Matisse worked on the design and decoration of the Chapel of the Rosary at Vence.

At Ronchamp a neo-Gothic church built in 1924 on a hill overlooking the sweeping but severe scenery of the Vosges had been destroyed in the war in 1944. The Archbishop of Besançon dispatched a delegation to ask Le Corbusier to build a replacement.

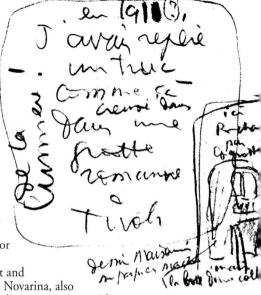

The external appearance of the pilgrimage church Notre-Dame-du-Haut at Ronchamp was settled from the moment the first sketch was made. But dozens of small sketches in Le Corbusier's notebooks bear witness to a long planning process. The architecture is complex and many references to earlier buildings can be discerned within it – for instance Hadrian's Villa at Tivoli, which inspired the tower 'light traps' on the roof of the chapel.

On his first visit to the site Le Corbusier made a sketch of an outline in one of his notebooks which already contained the essential features of the plan. The chapel is a complex arrangement of interlocking parts, but the exterior aspect is of a single body, full of energy, visible on its hilltop from all sides. The pews and crucifix were carved by Joseph Savina, the Breton cabinet maker with whose collaboration Le Corbusier produced all his sculpture. Close to the chapel, Le Corbusier built a house for the caretaker and a pilgrims' hostel.

Like Le Corbusier's other architecture, but to an even greater extent, Ronchamp unfolds as the spectator walks around it. He said, 'Good architecture "walks" and "moves", inside as well as outside. It is living architecture.'

Although based on the shape of a cross, the plan is asymmetrical. A framework of concrete beams and columns supports a roof in the shape of a hollow shell (or a thick aeroplane wing); Le Corbusier claimed to have been inspired by a crab shell. The roof extends well beyond the walls, which are convexly curved and (in places) sloping. Vosges stone from the bombed prior church was re-used in the walls. Three secondary chapels bear high concrete caps which look like the ventilation shafts of a passenger ship. The location of the chapel on the crown of a hill, surrounded by fields, and the open-air pulpit allow services for the congregation and large numbers of pilgrims to be held outside.

Except for the concrete roof shell, Notre-Dame-du-Haut at Ronchamp is covered in white roughcast. The walls are decorated with various sculptural features: small windows with coloured glass painted by Le Corbusier, a gargoyle and a basin for collecting rainwater, an outside pulpit. The door is covered with steel plates with designs by the architect enamelled in the Jean Martin workshop in Luynes. The variety of curved shapes make an attractive sight, yet produce a kind of lyrical tension. The sense of spirituality conferred on this simple chapel by Le Corbusier makes it one of the great religious buildings of the 20th century. 'Architecture is an event that suddenly emerges from the mind or soul of the architect: he may be preoccupied with making the building solid, or meeting demands for comfort, when suddenly he finds himself uplifted by a desire to do more than simply meet needs – he wants to express lyrical forces that give us joy.'

The Duval factory, the Currutchet and Jaoul houses

While he was working on the *Unité d'habitation* in Marseilles, Le Corbusier also designed a number of other projects, among them the Duval factory at Saint-Dié (1946–50), a house for Dr Currutchet in Buenos Aires (1949) and the Jaoul houses at Neuilly-sur-Seine (1951–5). Each marked a step forward for his architecture, individually and in their particular contexts.

The keynote of the Duval factory is functionalism, and it is the first of Le Corbusier's buildings in which sun-screens are integral to the construction. The local pink sandstone is used on the windowless gable ends

Inside Ronchamp Le Corbusier manipulated light, 'architecture's palette', with great skill. Light pours into the chapel through the painted glass of the odd shaped little windows, through the 'caps' over the secondary chapels and through the gap between the supporting walls and the roof.

The Jaoul houses (left) were built in Neuilly to house two families. The ground plans are almost identical: main rooms giving on to the garden, bedrooms upstairs. All the proportions are based on the Modulor formula developed in 1947. The framework consists of three load-bearing walls forming two parallel spans. The outside combines wood, brick and roughcast concrete.

and contrasts with the roughcast concrete of the façade. The Currutchet house combines Purist elements with elements adapted to the local climate. The façades of the Jaoul houses, a combination of brick and concrete, mark Le Corbusier's transition into the so-called 'brutalist' phase (a style based on the use of unmoulded concrete, 'béton brut') that he first introduced in the Duval factory. The lowered ceilings are tiled in 'Catalan vaults' which lend intimacy to the interiors.

Chandigarh: an invitation from Nehru

The major commission undertaken in the last ten years of Le Corbusier's life came from India. The state of Punjab, created by the partition of India and Pakistan in 1947, required the development of a capital, to be called Chandigarh. The prime minister of India, Pandit Nehru, first asked Albert Mayer, the American architect, for a plan for the new town. However, Matthew Nowicki, Mayer's Polish assistant in charge of his public commissions, was killed in a plane crash and the contract came to nothing. In 1950 Nehru dispatched P. N. Thapar, the state administrator, and P. Varma, the chief engineer, to Europe. There they met the English

Jean-Jacques Duval was a manufacturer whose hosiery factory had been partially destroyed during the war; he commissioned Le Corbusier to rebuild it in 1946. The architect designed a three-storey building raised on a double row of *pilotis*, topped with a roof terrace housing the offices. In a layout similar to that of the Pavillon Suisse in the Cité Universitaire in Paris, Le Corbusier installed the entrance hall and staircase in a separate block. The south side has the first *brise-soleil* (sun-screen) built in France, just pre-dating the screen on the *Unité d'habitation* in Marseilles.

Pandit Nehru, the first prime minister of the modern nation of India, wanted the new Punjabi capital city to make a mark. His invitation to Le Corbusier is evidence of his desire for modernity. In response to his wishes Le Corbusier designed a progressive city. The brief that he was given, however, did not really allow him fully to apply his theories on modern town planning. He favoured high-density building in the city centre, whereas buildings in Chandigarh are scattered. The large highways are designed to carry heavy vehicular traffic, but the bicycle remains the most popular form of transport. The administrative centre, lacking any commercial

architects Maxwell Fry and Jane Drew, both members of the CIAM, who suggested that they contact Le Corbusier. The project presented exceptional problems but, after some hesitation, Le Corbusier accepted and in November 1950 was appointed its chief consultant.

He designated three architects to supervise work on site, Maxwell Fry, Jane Drew and his cousin Pierre Jeanneret, with whom he was working again after a long interval and who played a crucial role in the construction of Chandigarh.

In 1951 he drew up the plan for the new city and on 22 November met Nehru and expressed his pleasure in the undertaking, commenting on his deep involvement, both intellectually and emotionally. He was already rather obsessed by the 'open-hand' motif he had developed, and told Nehru that he wanted to include a sculpture of it in the plan.

activity, seems disproportionately large. Above: the planned open-hand monument was not erected until 1986, just before the centenary of the architect's birth.

Le Corbusier

Les "Taureaux"

Ozons, Ubus and Bulls

Le Corbusier's intense activity as an architect did not interfere with the development of his painting and sculpture. In his view the different forms of expression were closely linked: 'It is in the practice of the plastic arts – "pure creation" – that I have found the intellectual stimulus for my town planning and my architecture.' Since the 1930s Le Corbusier had been working towards a 'synthesis of the arts'. In 1949 he became the first vice-president of the 'Association pour la synthèse des arts plastiques', whose president was Henri Matisse. The second vice-president was André Bloc, founder of the magazine *L'Architecture d'aujourd'hui*, and Picasso was a member. Several times Le Corbusier put forward plans for a house devoted to the synthesis of all the arts, without success. The Maison de l'Homme in Zurich, however, was constructed to his designs after his death, thanks to the Swiss architect Heidi Weber.

As a young man Charles-Edouard Jeanneret had wanted to become a painter. Later in life Le Corbusier was disappointed that his

In the 1950s Le Corbusier began a series of paintings in very bright colours with tortured and sometimes brutal shapes, drawn from various sources. His approach had grown more complex; in *Le Poème de l'angle droit*, Le Corbusier provides a key to part of it: 'The elements of a painting are gathered from all quarters; this time the key elements are a stump of dead wood and a pebble, both picked up in a lane in the Pyrenees. Oxen passed by my window all day long. After being drawn over and over again, the ox, made of the pebble and root, became a bull.' He did different versions on enamelled steel plates (below).

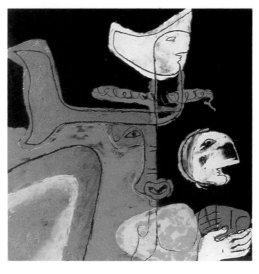

painting was appreciated less than his architecture. Nevertheless, he had several large one-man exhibitions, at the Institute of Contemporary Art in Boston in 1948,

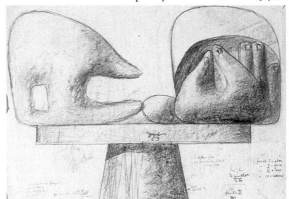

The collaboration between Le Corbusier and Savina (below) was remarkable. In 1936 the architect drew some sketches of furniture for the Breton cabinet maker, whom he had met in a friend's house. They persuaded Savina to deviate from the Breton tradition. After the war Savina sent Le Corbusier small sculptures he had made from the architect's sketches, and so began a long partnership.

at the Musée National d'Art Moderne and the Galerie Denise René in Paris in 1953, and at the Kunsthalle in Berne in 1954.

After his Purist years, and the period when his subjects aimed to provoke a 'poetic reaction', Le Corbusier started introducing a more elaborate range of subjects into his work in 1940. The series of *Ozons* and *Ubus*, then the *Bulls* series, contain complex forms. Colours are richer, sometimes quite violent. Planes cut across one another, objects and figures are distorted. Dreams and imagination transform reality, clearly

From 1956 to 1957 Le Corbusier produced a series of coloured drawings, then a painting, depicting the head and upper body of a woman with large hands in the foreground. From these he created several sculptures: *The Hands* (above left) and a series of female figures (right).

revealing the influence of Surrealism. The paintings and drawings are often preparatory to the sculpture.

Acoustic sculpture

In 1938 Le Corbusier had proposed a monument in memory of Pierre Vaillant-Couturier, the communist deputy who was editor of *L'Humanité* from 1929 to 1937; it was to be erected in Villejuif, just outside Paris, but was never made and Le Corbusier had lost interest in the project.

In 1946 a Breton cabinet maker and sculptor, Joseph Savina, whom

Le Corbusier had known for about ten years, sent the architect a small figure copied from one of his drawings. Le Corbusier was interested at once in his work and a collaboration began between the two men that was to last for nearly twenty years. Their working method was unusual: Le Corbusier drew and explained, more often than not in writing, between trips abroad, and Savina translated and interpreted. Forty-four sculptures in various woods were born from the collaboration, signed by both Le Corbusier and Savina. They are generally small in size, except for the *Totem* of 1950 and the *Woman* of 1953. Some of them are left a natural colour, others polychromed by Le Corbusier.

Sculpture was an essential mode of expression for him. The interplay of surfaces and volumes, of mass and void, represents the same kind of interplay of forces and tensions as in a building; like a building or a group of buildings, a sculpture 'radiates' into the space around it. Le Corbusier talked of 'acoustic sculpture' which transmits and receives. Free from the constraints – of site, time-scale, clients, finance – imposed upon architecture, sculpture provided another way of inhabiting and moulding space.

The 'nomadic mural'

Le Corbusier had created his first tapestry in 1936 at the request of Marie Cuttoli, a patron of tapestry weaving. He did not take up this kind of work again until 1948, when he made about thirty cartoons for tapestries, twenty-eight of which were executed. Some, like the tapestries for the Parliament Building and the Courts of Justice in Chandigarh or a stage curtain for Tokyo, were very large. Decisive in his return to tapestry design after the war was a meeting with Pierre Baudouin, a teacher at the art school in Aubusson and himself a painter, who taught Le Corbusier tapestry techniques to help him make the transition from a reduced-scale sketch to a full-scale cartoon, and from the cartoon to a finished work, woven by the tapestry weavers.

Le Corbusier was quick to recognize in tapestry a powerful means of expression to which his sense of built space, in particular wall space, responded keenly. He referred to tapestry as a 'nomadic mural' because it is a wall of wool that can be taken down, rolled up and hung elsewhere, whenever its owner moves on. The density and texture of the fabric appealed to his taste. He had eight tapestries, each measuring 64 square metres (688 square feet), made for the Courts of Justice in Chandigarh, and another that measured 144 square metres (1550 square feet); he used them to modify the austerity of raw concrete walls and to improve the acoustics in the council chambers.

Modulor

As a young man he had striven to understand the equilibrium of forms and the harmonies created by space and mass. He showed an early interest in 'regulating lines' and proportion, analysing the composition of classical buildings and transferring their proportions to the façades of his Purist buildings. In 1943 he extended the scope of his theorizing, constructing a grid of harmonizing measurements in an attempt to establish a series of relating sizes linked by the Golden Section. The mathematician Leonardo Fibonacci had, in the 13th century, created a sequence of harmonic numbers, bearing his name, based on a mathematical progression; now Le Corbusier created a

In tapestry Le Corbusier discovered an art form with applications to architecture; unlike the interior walls of a house, a tapestry can move with its owners. He used all his favourite themes: women, hands, ropework. Below: his colours are intense and include a lot of red, as here in *Woman on a Red Background* (1965). Opposite: his large sculpture *Totem* (1950).

grid based on the proportions of the human body. This was a notion already explored in the 1930s by Matila Ghyka. 'Its great advantage is this: the human body as an accepted support to a system of numbers.… That's proportion! Proportion puts order into our relationship with our environment'.

Le Corbusier named his system 'Modulor' during a conference in 1947. In 1950 he published a book describing his methods of research and his results: *Le Modulor: Essai sur une mesure harmonique à l'échelle humaine applicable universellement à l'architecture et à la mécanique*. (The Modulor: A Harmonious Measure on the Human Scale Universally Applicable to Architecture and Mechanics). In 1955 a second book, *Modulor 2*, appeared, summarizing the process.

The figure of a standing man, on which the grid was constructed, became internationally famous. Once he had worked out the system, Le Corbusier determined the measurements of all his constructions according to the Modulor. The 'human proportions' of the *Unité d'Habitation* in Marseilles are based on these principles.

La Charte d'Athènes and other writings

On the identity card issued to him by the Paris police, after his naturalization,

Modulor: Le Corbusier created a series of harmonic numbers; one was the average height of a human being (initially 1.75 metres – 5 foot 7 inches – later 1.829 metres – 6 feet), the other the height of a man with raised arms. Several of the measurements were taken from other positions.

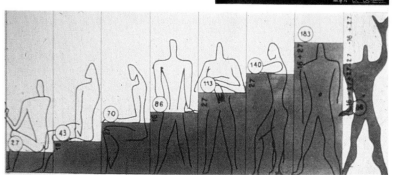

Although he was often begged to direct courses, Le Corbusier never wanted to teach. Roger Aujame came with other students to ask him to open a studio at the Ecole des Beaux Arts, but to no avail. As a self-taught man, who had satisfied his thirst for knowledge by himself, Le Corbusier held all schools in deep suspicion and distrusted the transmission of any knowledge that was not rooted in practical reality. But he had a taste for debate and enjoyed airing his ideas and seeking to persuade. He lectured throughout his career, sometimes on long tours (like the one to South America in 1929) organized for the purpose. The strong popularity of his appearances was not due to any outstanding gifts as a speaker but to the clarity of his expression, the strength of his convictions and his stimulating and provocative imagery. His skill as a communicator drew ever-increasing audiences; he honed his lecture technique over the years. He would pin large sheets of paper behind him and illustrate his talks on them as he went along, drawing in black and white or colour.

Charles-Edouard Jeanneret, 'known as Le Corbusier' gives his profession as 'man of letters'. Did he want to conceal the fact that he was an architect? Was he expressing a deeply felt aspiration? He did, in fact, produce some forty books, as well as a large number of articles, introductions to books and so on.

Le Corbusier's written work consists mainly of manifestos, or presentations of his ideas and his architecture. In 1943 he published *Entretien avec les étudiants des écoles d'architecture*, in 1945 *Les Trois Etablissements humains*, in 1946 *Manière de penser l'urbanisme* and in 1954 *Une petite maison*.

In *La Charte d'Athènes*, published in 1943, Le Corbusier reiterates conclusions reached at the fourth International Congress on Modern Architecture held in 1933.

When the book appeared, the ideas it put forward were virtually inadmissible. Many of them have since become so commonplace that in the reality of today's cities they seem laughably obvious.

Le Poème de l'angle droit consists of 19 lithographs and a lithographed text; its recurrent themes are: cosmic forces, the sun's course, man and woman, his wife, Yvonne, the Creation. One of the plates

Débarrassée d'entraves mieux qu'auparavant la maison des hommes maîtresse de sa forme s'installe dans la nature Entière en soi faisant son affaire de tout sol

Poésie sur Alger and *Le Poème de l'angle droit*

Le Corbusier had the gift of expressing himself clearly, using striking metaphors and a neat juxtaposition of word and image. After his two major manifestos, *Vers une architecture* and *L'Art décoratif d'aujourd'hui*, shorter works like his *Entretien avec les étudiants des écoles d'architecture* or *Une petite maison* demonstrate his communication skills. His responsive nature, the freedom with which he expressed himself and his strong sense of metaphor led him almost inevitably towards

represents four of the 'five points of the new architecture': *pilotis*, roof terrace, free plan, free façade – only the horizontal window is missing. The owl has borrowed the architect's large spectacles.

poetry. *Poésie sur Alger*, published in 1950, makes this inclination clear in the title, yet in reality is an account of the problems facing the town planner in the north African French colony of Algiers, then undergoing considerable modernization, and a defence of the seven plans the architect had drawn up, all of which had been rejected. In glowing terms, Le Corbusier expresses his feelings for the city 'where the sea, the Atlas Mountains and the hills of Kabylia unfurl their blue panoply'.

Le Poème de l'angle droit, published in 1955, makes a similar statement about its form. The images and text speak to each other, sometimes wildly and excitedly, sometimes lyrically and tenderly. Le Corbusier, then aged sixty-eight, never gave up confrontation: 'Go away come back go away again and fight struggle never stop being a soldier.' But the old soldier then seems suddenly struck by uncertainty: 'Shall we not be living on the side-lines of our lives?'

Frustration and disappointment, from the UN to UNESCO, from Algiers to Saint-Dié

Le Corbusier achieved a great deal, but also suffered a number of disappointments. His designs for international organizations – the League of Nations building in Geneva in 1927, the UN headquarters in New York in 1947 and the UNESCO building in Paris in 1951 – three of his largest projects, were either dismissed out of hand, changed beyond recognition or ignored. Apart from his plans for the Frugès district in Pessac and Chandigarh, little of his town-planning work was taken seriously. Le Corbusier was frequently embittered by this lack of recognition, but continued to press on doggedly with his work.

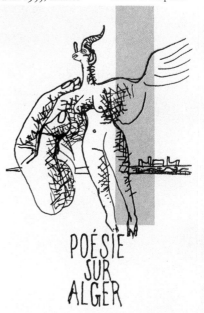

Poésie sur Alger is a curious work. In fifty pages Le Corbusier extols the grandeur of the city of Algiers and its site, to sum up thirteen years of meditation on the subject of urban planning and to express his bitterness at the failure of the public authorities to plan seriously for the future. The architect's character is captured in these powerful, resonant pages, with their sense of mixed naïveté and regret.

During the final ten years of his lifetime, Le Corbusier wrote and painted much less, but produced the bulk of his sculpture and tapestry. Most of his energy was devoted to architecture. The crowning achievements of the period are the monumental buildings at Chandigarh and the monastery at La Tourette. The French government decided to commission another public project from him, though he only had time to make preliminary sketches for the plan before he died.

CHAPTER 5

FULFILMENT

The involvement of Nehru, the sheer scale of the buildings and the significance of their functions – political, legal, administrative – gave the Chandigarh project exceptional international importance.

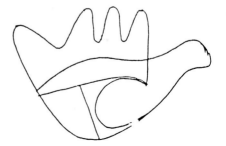

In 1957 Le Corbusier mourned the death of his wife, Yvonne: 'A woman with exceptional qualities of warmth and good nature, of integrity and decency. The guardian of the hearth, my hearth, for thirty-six years'. He had been deeply attached to her. Her sense of fun had certainly helped him through problems and disappointments over the years. In *Le Poème de l'angle droit* Le Corbusier is evidently thinking of Yvonne (although he does not name her) when he writes: 'I find my reflection in her. She has grandeur without knowing it. Who made her thus? Where did she come from? The uprightness of a child with a pure heart, standing here on earth beside me. The simplest everyday acts reflect the nobility of her soul.'

In 1959 Le Corbusier lost his mother, by now over one hundred years old. He held her in a special kind of veneration, writing of her, when she was ninety-one, that she still reigned in majesty at 'La Petite Maison', 'ruling the stars, the moon, the mountains, the lake and the household, surrounded by the affection of her admiring family.'

Ahmedabad

While he was working on the first plans for the new capital of Punjab, Le Corbusier took on some commissions in Ahmedabad, a large and ancient city in western India. In the space of a few years he designed the Shodhan and Sarabhai villas, a museum and the headquarters of the wool weavers' association. These buildings, with their angular shapes and generalized use of reinforced concrete, are examples of brutalist architecture. For Le Corbusier they provided a useful opportunity to experiment with construction methods and to learn something about the constraints imposed on architecture by the Indian climate, before the construction of the public buildings in Chandigarh.

Villa Shodhan in Ahmedabad (1952–4): Le Corbusier took his lead from traditional Indian design, adapting the elements he had been developing since the 1920s to the hot, humid local climate. A shade-giving roof covers the whole building, and wide, deep-set sun-screens protect the rooms from sun and light whilst allowing fresh air to circulate. Terraces and ramps in roughcast concrete contrast with the tropical vegetation in the garden.

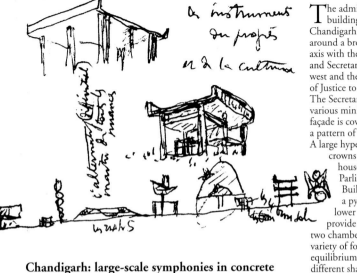

The administrative buildings of Chandigarh are grouped around a broad central axis with the Parliament and Secretariat to the west and the Courts of Justice to the east. The Secretariat houses various ministries. The façade is covered with a pattern of sun-screens. A large hyperbola crowns the upper house of the Parliament Building, and a pyramid the lower house; they provide light for the two chambers. The great variety of forms, the equilibrium among the different shapes, the interplay of columns, terraces, ramps and sun-screens, the reflection of the buildings in water and the use of colour confer a monumental and dynamic quality on the whole that has seldom been equalled.

Chandigarh: large-scale symphonies in concrete

The plans for Chandigarh show five large public buildings in the administrative centre, to the north of the city. Only three of these have been built, the Parliament Building, the Courts of Justice and the Secretariat. Two others, the state governor's residence and a museum, are still in the planning stage and their absence disturbs the balance of the whole composition.

After his disappointments over the plans for great public buildings in Geneva and Moscow, Le Corbusier at last had the chance to design a complex on a monumental scale. Although his city is planned around a central axis, Le Corbusier, now consummate master of his art, orchestrates the grouping of his buildings asymmetrically, shifting frontages and breaking up straight lines. The buildings, never conventionally aligned, present a great variety of aspects and dimensions. The ensemble is evidently inspired by the great classical town plans but, thanks to the architect's games with symmetry, has a dynamic quite unlike those models.

The open spaces are based on Modulor proportions, but are landscaped with ditches and hillocks, pools of water and

Chandigarh is divided into sectors with the business area in the centre, the industrial zone near the station and the administrative centre in the north. The roads, the '7 vs', are ranked according to importance: from 1 for major through routes to 7 for pedestrian streets. Children do not have to cross any roads between home and school.

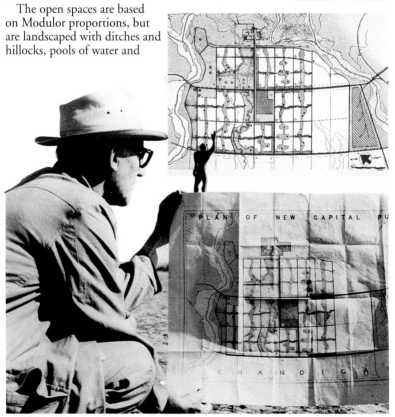

occasional pieces of sculpture. The carefully structured landscaping links the buildings and space into an integrated network of interdependent areas. Once again, in his treatment of open spaces, Le Corbusier shows that 'the outside is also an inside', that the space between buildings is also part of their architecture. Such space should not be treated randomly but should be designed coherently and in a structured way, with built elements enclosing or featuring in it. The link with his 'acoustic sculpture' is obvious here: volumes, masses and voids are handled in such a manner that they 'transmit' and 'receive' messages to and from one another.

The Parliament Building, Courts of Justice and Secretariat are closely related visually in their uniform use of roughcast concrete, but differ widely in their shapes. Some of the concrete elements of the various buildings have a quality that is virtually sculptural: the curves of the canopies, the openings pierced in concrete screen walls, loggias, gargoyles, ramps, superstructures on the flat rooftops, together read as an assemblage. Inside the buildings, to cope with the strength of the Indian sun and feature the distant view of the Himalayas across the plain, Le Corbusier controlled and filtered light with more than usual care. His obsession with the image of the human hand is evident everywhere – in his drawings, his paintings, his tapestry

The Courts of Justice building (above) in Chandigarh has a framework of large columns and arches supporting a sunshade roof. The western façade is partially occupied by the main entrance; this and the sun-screens are reflected in a pool. The rectangular façade (based on Modulor) is transformed into a square. Access to the upper floors is by several flights of a long ramp. Open corridors allow fresh air to circulate. Coloured paint emphasizes the upward thrust of the big pylons and enlivens the sun-screens.

and sculpture. He wanted to provide Chandigarh with a focal point in the shape of a large sculpture of the open hand, rotating in the wind, built above an open air amphitheatre, or 'contemplation pit', with a view towards the Himalayas. This project was only realized after his death. He himself designed and built some minor buildings in the Punjabi capital: a museum, a yacht club and a school of art and architecture.

The monastery of La Tourette: brutalism and virtuosity

At the suggestion of Père Couturier, who had already played his part in the selection of Le Corbusier for the chapel at Ronchamp, the provincial chapter of the Dominicans at Lyons put forward Le Corbusier's name in 1952 for the construction of a monastery at Eveux-sur-l'Arbresle, about thirty kilometres (eighteen miles) from Lyons. Designs were produced in 1953, building work began in 1956 and the monastery was completed in 1959. Construction was carried out with medieval thoroughness.

The simplicity of the shapes and the extreme roughness of the concrete are in sharp contrast to the subtle arrangement of the interior space, the variety of window openings and the quality of light, direct or reflected, inside. The monastery is built on a barren site, but achieves a high degree of spirituality. At Ronchamp, Le Corbusier, an agnostic with a Protestant background,

The plan of the monastery of La Tourette was inspired by Cistercian architecture. The square building is supported on a sloping site by a foundation of *pilotis*. The chapel is built on a succession of levels and receives natural light from three 'cannons of light' on the roof, surmounted by truncated cones.

presented the Catholic Church with a dazzling white chapel, conducive (with its enfolding curves) to prayer. At La Tourette he provided the Dominican friars with an austere environment suitable for study, meditation and spiritual reflection.

Last projects, last work

While Chandigarh was being built and La Tourette completed, Le Corbusier put the finishing touches to a number of projects in Europe, America and Asia. For the Brussels Exhibition in 1958 he designed, with the

The monastery fills three sides of the square and the church the fourth. Two storeys contain the monks' cells, one the entrance and meeting hall and one the communal areas – the refectory and the chapter house. As at Ema, the cells open to the exterior by overhanging loggias.

The only building in the United States built to Le Corbusier's design – the Carpenter Centre for the Visual Arts (left), Cambridge, Mass., is a square central block with two large curved auditoria, one on each side. An S-shaped ramp crosses from one side of the building to the other, inviting the students to take an 'architectural promenade'.

assistance of Yannis Xenakis, the Philips Pavilion. In 1959, in collaboration with two Japanese architects, Maekawa and Sakakura, who had worked in his office in the Rue de Sèvres before setting up their own practice in Japan, he built the Museum of Western Art in Tokyo. In the same year, with Lucio Costa, he built the Pavillon du Brésil in the Cité Universitaire in Paris.

In 1962 Josep Lluís Sert, who had also worked with Le Corbusier at an earlier date, invited him, on behalf of

Le Corbusier made several studies for pavilions devoted to all the arts. The Maison de l'Homme (1964) is built on a metal framework and is covered by an oversized detached steel roof. This centre in Zurich was constructed in 1967 (below) thanks to Heidi Weber.

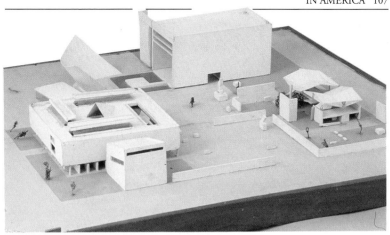

the Graduate School of Design at Harvard University (of which he was dean) to build the Carpenter Center for the Visual Arts, in Cambridge, Massachusetts. The architect's brief was very vague, perhaps because such an institution was a novelty, or perhaps because Sert had absolute confidence in Le Corbusier's abilities. Whatever the explanation, the function of the accommodation had to be considered at the same time as its physical plan.

If the maxim of the American architect Louis Sullivan – 'form follows function' – really means what it is generally held to mean, that form 'flows' from function, the architecture being more or less determined by the building's purpose, then the Carpenter Center could be held up as an illustration of its truth. The absence of a clear brief seems to have deprived the architect of an essential spur to his invention. Le Corbusier re-used a number of his favourite themes – *pilotis*, ramps, sunscreens. The concrete is exposed but, unusually, has been smoothed and 'softened', apparently at the express request of the architect.

In 1955 Eugène Claudius Petit, a loyal friend and supporter of Le Corbusier and deputy mayor of Firminy, a small industrial town about ten kilometres (six miles) from Saint-Etienne, asked the architect to construct the largest collection of buildings that he

Le Corbusier conceived in 1939 the idea of a museum that could be extended in an unlimited number of ways. It was to consist of a series of galleries on columns, arranged in a spiral around a central area; the gallery space, based on the shape of a mollusc shell, would expand as the collection grew. The wall space would be continuous, with light entering from above. In the Museum of Western Art in Tokyo (above) Le Corbusier designed galleries wrapped around a central space, but a small building at the back of the galleries (apparently added after the completion of the main buildings) would preclude any further extension.

would ever have designed on French soil: a sports stadium, cultural centre, church and a residential area. The cultural centre was the only building of the group completed before his death. The sports centre and the residential area were later finished by André Wogenscky and Fernand Gardien.

Le Corbusier started working on the church in 1960, in collaboration with José Oubrerie. He had designed a church at Le Tremblay in 1929, and the underground Basilique de la Sainte-Baume in 1945–51, neither of which was built; then the chapel at Ronchamp and the monastery at La Tourette.

At Firminy he approached religious architecture in quite a different spirit, designing a totally new kind of church. Construction began in 1970, five years after the architect's death, but was halted for financial reasons. Eugène Claudius Petit campaigned tirelessly, right up to his death in 1989, for the completion of the church. However, in spite of his efforts and his approaches to the highest authorities he never managed to raise the funds to finish the project.

Eugène Claudius Petit, mayor of Firminy from 1957 to 1971, commissioned Le Corbusier in 1955 to design an extension to 'Firminy Vert', including several public buildings. The Maison de la Culture (above and right) is built on a high part of the site and has a sloping façade that overhangs the sportsground.

From the cabin at Cap Martin to the Cour Carrée of the Louvre

In 1962, when he was over seventy-five and working with Julian de la Fuente on the preliminary stages of the design for a hospital in Venice, Le Corbusier was asked by André Malraux, the then minister of culture, to design a huge arts complex at La Défence, on the western edge of Paris. The complex was to consist of a museum of 20th-century art and four educational establishments, for the applied arts, architecture, music and dance, and cinema and television. By awarding this great public project, of national importance, to Le Corbusier, the French government at last showed signs of recognizing his creative genius. Le Corbusier had his doubts about the site from the outset, and tried to persuade Malraux to demolish the Grand Palais, so that its site could be used. However, before he had had time to make more than a few quick sketches, he died and the project had to be abandoned.

If the church at Firminy had been finished it would have been Le Corbusier's third religious building, after Ronchamp and La Tourette. At Firminy a square plan on four levels is entered via a ramp. The church itself occupies the two upper levels, under a truncated cone. The interior spaces are integrated with the utmost fluidity. The four sides of the lower part have three concrete abutments, each providing light to the church through a slit. They support the huge cone and give an overall impression of lightness.

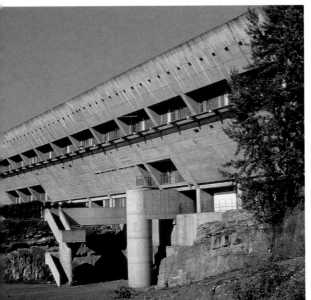

In 1951 Le Corbusier had a small cabin built for him at Cap Martin, facing the sea and Monaco. The restaurant *L'Etoile de mer*, run by the Rebutato family, where Le Corbusier used to eat his meals, was nearby, and the villa built in 1929 by Eileen Gray and Jean Badovici, decorated with frescoes by Le Corbusier, not far off. The architect spent every summer in his cabin thinking, drawing and writing, away from the hustle and bustle and stress of the office. The sea was very close and he spent a lot of his time swimming.

In July 1965 Le Corbusier went down to Cap Martin for his holiday as usual. Although his family were worried about his health, which did not seem too good, he wrote to his brother on 24 August: 'Dear old Albert...I've never been so fit.' Nevertheless, on 27 August 1965, when he was swimming in the Mediterranean he loved so much, he died suddenly. For one night his body rested before the altar in the church of the monastery at La Tourette, and on 1 September it was taken to Paris.

For the last time Le Corbusier entered his office at 35 Rue de Sèvres. The French authorities decided to give

While he was staying with Eileen Gray and Jean Badovici at Cap Martin, Le Corbusier made the acquaintance of the Rebutato brothers (above). In 1951 he decided to build a log cabin near their restaurant; it was built by Barbéris, his Corsican joiner, who had the elements prefabricated in Ajaccio. The cabin is a square hut with measurements from Modulor: 3.66 metres (12 feet) by 3.66 metres (12 feet) and 2.26 metres (7½ feet) high. It uses minimal space in an exemplary fashion and is much sought out by architects interested in the design of holiday homes.

him a state funeral. That evening, after dark, in the illuminated Cour Carrée of the Louvre, in front of thousands of mourners, André Malraux made a subdued but heartfelt speech.

Le Corbusier had always realized (and had recently committed it to paper) that 'it takes at least twenty years for an idea to be recognized, thirty for it to be implemented – by which time it should have been superseded'; and 'it is then that plaudits, and eulogies and commemorative plaques start raining down. It is too late.'

The tiny village of Roquebrune-Cap-Martin possesses one of those seaside cemeteries from which one can gaze over the Mediterranean to the hazy horizon. Le Corbusier designed the tomb that was to hold his ashes and the ashes of his wife Yvonne, who died in 1957. A low plinth, a modified cube, a cylinder: space, precision, geometry.

DOCUMENTS

'Perseverance, hard work and courage
are all important. There are no glorious
signals in the sky.
Courage is an interior strength,
and courage alone can define
the quality of an existence.'
Le Corbusier, 1965

Education and training, revolt, rejection of school

In 1908 the young Charles-Edouard Jeanneret was working in the Paris office of the brothers Perret, where he came across a new attitude to architecture and the architect, very different from the teachings of his old tutor, Charles l'Eplattenier, whom he held in affection.

The studio in the Rue Jacob, Paris.

In a long letter to L'Eplattenier, written on Sunday, 22 November 1908, Charles-Edouard Jeanneret discusses his ideas and his regrets.

My dear Maître,

…Maybe you were not wrong when you made me something other than an engraver, because *I feel that I am strong.*

I need not remind you that my life is not one of pleasure, but of intense, essential work. To become an architect from being an engraver (as I used to be), because of the concept of the particular profession that I hold, is a very big step….

I've got forty years ahead of me to achieve what I am just beginning to sketch out on my clean slate….

My concept of the art of building is based on the fundamentals, all that my insufficient (or incomplete) resources have so far allowed me to master.

Vienna killed off my interest in form as the main component of architecture. When I arrived in Paris I felt a great emptiness inside me, and I said to myself, 'Poor thing! You don't know

anything yet and, worse still, you don't know what it is you don't know.' That was what caused me such bitter anxiety. Who could I ask? Chapallaz knew even less than I did and increased my confusion. Grasset, then F. Jourdain, Sauvage, Paquet – I saw Perret but I did not dare question him. All these people said to me: 'You know enough about architecture already'. My spirit rebelled and I went off to consult the past. I chose the most *impassioned* fighters, who we in the 20th century would most like to resemble: the builders of the Romanesque period. For three months I studied the Romanesque every evening in the library. I went to Notre-Dame and followed the last part of Magne's course on Gothic art at the Beaux-Arts, and I learned to understand.

After that it was the Perret brothers who spurred me on. They castigated me: at work and sometimes in conversation they would say: 'You know nothing'. My studies of the Romanesque persuaded me that architecture is not simply about harmony of form, but...something else...but what? I wasn't sure. I studied mechanics, then statics; I spent a whole summer sweating over that. I've made so many mistakes, and now I realize with horror just how many gaps there are in my knowledge of modern architecture. With horror and joy, because *at last I realize* what is worthwhile. I am studying forces: it's tough, but maths is beautiful, so logical and perfect!...

On the Perrets' construction sites I have been observing concrete, its composition and the revolutionary forms that it demands. My eight months in Paris cry out to me: logic, truth, away with dreams of the art of the past. Lift up your eyes and go forward! Paris says to me, loud and unmistakeably, 'Burn

the things you used to love, then worship what you burnt'....

An architect must have a logical brain in his head; he needs to be wary of superficial effects; he must be a scientist with a heart, an artist and scholar. *I know it*, and none of you told me. Ancestors will speak to you if you know how to consult them....

People talk about an art of tomorrow. This art *will come*. Because mankind's way of living, his way of thinking, has changed. The programme is new. It is new, in a new setting, we can talk about an art of the future because the new setting is iron, iron is the new medium. The dawn of this art is breaking, and it is because iron, which is destructible, has created reinforced concrete, a material producing incredible results. In the history of monumental architecture this is going to mark a milestone of courage....

I shall no longer be in agreement with you if things do not change. I could not be. Your aim to turn young men of twenty into mature, *active* executives (they execute and assume responsibilities, with their successors and heirs in mind). *You*, at the height of your creative powers, imagine that the young have already reached the same height. The power *is there*; but it needs to be developed in the direction that you, unconsciously (because today you seem to deny your young life) were developing it in Paris and on your journeys, and in your first lonely years in La Chaux-de-Fonds....

I say that this small success is premature; ruin is nigh. We should not build on sand. The movement took off too late. Your soldiers are ghosts. When the battle starts *you will be alone*. Your soldiers are ghosts because they don't know they exist, or why they exist, or how they exist. Your soldiers have never thought. The art of tomorrow will be an art of thought.

Concept to the fore, and ever upwards!…

I remain your affectionate student.

Le Corbusier was largely self-taught, and he was the committed adversary of all schools and academies. He explains his position in a book written on his return from the USA in 1937, Quand les cathédrales étaient blanches, *translated as* When the Cathedrals were White.

Schools are the product of 19th-century theories. They have brought about immense progress in the domain of the exact sciences; they have warped activities dependent on imagination, for they have fixed 'canons', the 'true' and 'right' rules, which are recognized, officially stamped, legally accepted. In an epoch of total disorder in which nothing today is like what it was yesterday, they have established an official break [*sic*] in the form of a 'diploma'; thus they are against life; they represent memory, security, lethargy. In particular, they have killed architecture by operating in a vacuum, far away from the weight of materials, the resistances of matter, the tremendous progress in the field of machinery. They have vilified crafts associated with matter, time, expense. Architecture has evaded life in place of being an expression of it. The distressing ugliness of the 19th and 20th centuries comes in a straight line from the schools. This ugliness is not the result of bad intentions; on the contrary it comes from incongruity, from incoherence, from the separation which occurs between the idea and its realization. Design has killed architecture. Design is what they teach in the schools. The leader of these

regrettable practices, the Ecole des Beaux-Arts in Paris, reigns in the midst of equivocation, endowed with a dignity which is only a usurpation of the creative spirit of earlier periods. It is the seat of the most disconcerting paradox, since under the ferule of extremely conservative methods, everything is good will, hard work, faith….

I admire the dazzling manual skill acquired by the students through the instruction of the Ecole des Beaux-Arts…. I could wish that the head might command the hand. I recognize the elegance which guides the solutions of plan, façade and section. But I should like to see intelligence dominating elegance and not being disregarded. I regret that the problems at the School are conceived outside of the condition of the craft and that it does not call upon modern technicians except to accomplish miracles of bad quality: in order to make things stand up which, otherwise, could never be constructed or which would fall down if the materials shown in the design were used. In this matter modern times, with a fearful waste of money, is reduced to playing the role of prop for thought which lacks bones and muscles, for thought with its arm in a sling. Thus was born the architecture in a sling of the Ecole des Beaux-Arts….

I think that this kind of instruction, in the sumptuary form of a supreme diploma – coronation – organized, moreover, in the shadow of the Institute is unacceptably pretentious in the midst of the great melee of modern times. Why should *vanity* be the appanage of the architect when architecture should never be vain, but healthy, just and worthy? Besides, in the new times architecture extends to the unprecedented mass of contemporary

Charles-Edouard Jeanneret photographed at home in the Rue Jacob in the 1920s.

productions. Where does architecture belong? In everything! *Shelter* – dwellings and means of transportation (roads, railways, water, air). *Equipment* – the city, the farm, the useful village, the port and also the furnishing of the house: domestic machinery. *Form* – everything that our hands touch or that our eyes see in this new world of materials and functional organisms which, in a hundred years, have so suddenly surrounded our life with plastic realities which are alive and palpitating in the light.

Shall we give, shall we demand diplomas for all the activities which have the right to relate themselves to architecture and which represent one of the largest parts of current activity? The world turned into diplomas? The question thus posed shows the ridiculousness of diplomas. We no longer need diplomas. The world is open, not closed.

The studious and painful conquest (I know that from the confidences of many young students) of the diploma demanded by the father or the family (poor people, they imagine that when their child leaves school he will be the beneficiary of exceptional rights in the apportionment of life), the winning of the diploma in four or six years absorbs the precious moments of youth, of generous malleability, of magnificent enthusiasm, of *opening* in the face of multifarious life. The diploma closes everything like a cork. It says: 'It is finished, you have stopped suffering and learning. Henceforth you are free!' The idea of *learning* has become synonymous with *suffering*! Youth is killed. Learning? That is the joy of every day, the ray of sunlight in life. I say that if throughout life we developed the generous faculty of learning, men would discover in it happiness itself – free, unlimited, never-failing happiness, happiness up to their last day. We would make men of a different kind: new men....

In all humility I should like to know why the French Government considers itself authorized to give diplomas. I thought that the function of government was to administer its own times and to lead people on the paths of an ever-changing life; and not to set up obstacles.

When the Cathedrals were White
Translated by Francis E. Hyslop, 1947

Two fundamental sources: nature and the past

Le Corbusier found two indispensable sources of inspiration in studying the past and in contemplating nature. He did not just want to admire ancient or vernacular buildings for their age – he hoped to understand their function, their logic and how they were built. In nature he tried to identify the forms, structure and materials of organic matter, from which he took inspiration for his painting and sculpture.

A watercolour of Venice by Le Corbusier.

In Entretien avec les étudiants des écoles d'architecture *(1943), Le Corbusier attempted to draw something vital and relevant from the lessons of the past.*

Carried away by my enthusiasm for defending the laws of invention, I took the past as my witness, the past which was my sole tutor and which continues to be my permanent mentor. A level-headed person, when launched into the uncharted waters of architectural invention, has no real choice but to pin his enthusiasm on to the lessons of bygone centuries. Those witnesses to the past that have survived the passing of the centuries possess eternal value for mankind. We could term them folklore, by which we mean the finest flower of popular tradition; their realm extends beyond houses for human beings, to houses for the gods. The finest flower, a link in the traditions they embody: each link in the chain represents a step forward that was, at the time, at least innovatory and often revolutionary; a contribution to civilization. History leans on steps such as these, but has only preserved these loyal witnesses; limitations, plagiarism, compromises are lined up behind, abandoned or even destroyed. Respect for the past is an attitude that comes naturally to those who create: it is the attitude of love and

respect of a son for his father. I will show you how much attention I paid to the study of folklore when I was young. Later, I campaigned with all my might to save the Casbah in Algiers, under threat of demolition because it sheltered too many crooks; also the Vieux Port in Marseilles which the ministry of transport decided in their wisdom should be turned into a junction for all the motorways of the South of France; old Barcelona, too, which gave me the chance of proposing a means of turning the heritage of cities to good account. None of this has prevented my detractors accusing me of wishing systematically to destroy the past.

You would not confuse this respect, love and admiration, however, with the insolence and indolence of a spoilt son who, to save himself effort, sells his clients the labours of his ancestors. Sadly, in this country, rational thought has been abandoned and we have been urged to put our cast-off traditional clothing back on again. A big group of the craven, the unimaginative, is getting ready to cover the town and countryside, the whole land, with architectural fakes. [The Athenian statesman] Solon would have punished such crimes. I was twenty-three when, after five months on the road, I reached the Parthenon in Athens. The pediment was still standing but the long side was on the ground, columns and entablatures toppled by the explosives stored there by the Turks. I spent several weeks handling these stones with reverence, concern, amazement. Standing up, at the correct height, they played one of the most impressive tunes in existence: a clarion call, eternal truths.

In L'Art décoratif d'aujourd'hui *(1925) the architect expresses his distrust of worshipping the past.*

The past is not infallible.… There were ugly things as well as beautiful. Bad taste was not born yesterday. The past has one advantage over the present: we have half forgotten it. The interest we take in it does not excite our active energies, which are violently engaged in the contemporary world, but it soothes our hours of leisure; we contemplate it with the benevolence of disinterest. Ethnographic significance, documentary importance, historical value, collectable value, all these are superimposed on its beauty or ugliness and, in either case, add to our interest. Our admiration for the artefacts of an earlier culture is thus often objective, a captivating encounter by our animal spirit with its own image lingering in the products of a developing culture: the simple human animal of a fun fair. Culture is a progression towards the inner life. Gilt decoration and precious stones are the work of the tamed savage who is still alive in us. No practical or elevated argument excuses or explains iconolatry. Since iconolatry thrives and spreads as virulently as a cancer, let us be iconoclasts.

The Decorative Art of Today
Translated by James I. Dunnett, 1987

In a letter written on 23 September 1936 to a group of architects in the Transvaal, Le Corbusier advocates the rejection of academicism in favour of inspiration taken directly from the observation of nature.

I don't think that enough notice is being taken of the fact that the world is in the melting pot – a new civilization is emerging that cannot be expressed by objects from the past. Everything must be new, everything must express this new state of consciousness. Study of the past can be fruitful provided you turn your back on academic teaching, if you extend your curiosity across the years, across space, to the civilizations, be they successful or modest, which gave fullest expression to human sensibility. Architecture has to be rescued from the drawing board, it has to be located in the heart and in the head. In the heart most of all, as a proof of love. To love what is appropriate, aware, inventive, varied. Reason is a guide, nothing more.

How can one's powers of creation be enhanced? Not surely by taking out a subscription to an architectural review, but by setting out on a voyage of discovery into the inexhaustible riches of the natural world. That's the real lesson to learn in architecture: grace, first and foremost. Yes, the suppleness, the precision, the inevitability of the couplings that nature offers to our gaze, always. From inside to outside: serene perfection. Plants, animals, trees, places, oceans, plains or mountains. Even the perfect harmony of natural catastrophes, geological cataclysm etc. Open your eyes! Get away from the straitjacket of narrow professional polemics. Involve yourself so deeply in the study of the essence of things that architecture is engendered spontaneously.

Smash the schools – the school of 'Corbu' just as much as the school of Vignola, I implore you. Reject formulae, reject gimmicks, reject sleight of hand. We are in the early stages of the architectural discovery of modern times. Fresh designs must spring up all over the place. In a hundred years' time we might talk of a 'style'. We cannot talk of 'a style' yet, but only of 'style', which means an honest, upright attitude to all that we create, we truly create.

I'd like architects (not only students) to pick up a pencil and draw a plant, a leaf, the skeleton of a tree, the rhythm of a shell, a cloud formation, the intricate pattern made by waves breaking on a beach. I'd like them to record the successive expressions of an inner force. I'd like their hands (and heads) to thrill to this intimate voyage of discovery.

On his return from America, Le Corbusier proclaimed his passion for trees in his book When the Cathedrals were White.

Trees are the friends of man, symbols of every organic creation; a tree is an image of a complete construction. A delightful spectacle which appears to us in the most fantastic, yet perfectly ordered arabesques; a mathematically measured play of branches multiplied each spring by a new life-giving hand. Leaves with finely placed nerves. A cover over us between earth and sky. A friendly screen close to our eyes. A pleasant measure interposed between our hearts and eyes and the eventual geometries of our hard constructions. A precious instrument in the hands of the city planner. The most concentrated expression of the forces of nature. The presence of nature in the city, surrounding our labours or our pleasures. Trees are the millenary companions of man!

Sun, space and *trees* are the fundamental materials of city planning, the bearers of the 'essential joys'. Considering them thus, I wished to restore urban man to the very heart of his natural setting, to his fundamental emotions. Deprived of trees, he exists with only the artificial frame of his own creations; it is proper that sometimes, on certain solemn occasions, he should affirm in all their rigour the purity and strength of his geometries. But deprived of trees in part or in the whole extent of cities in innumerable cases where nothing is planned, where everything is disagreeable and brutal, it is sad to be thus naked and impoverished, lost in the insecurity of a faltering order, in the arbitrariness of a fatal disorder.

Nevertheless, Central Park has been saved, in the middle of Manhattan.

You like to accuse Americans of being concerned only with making money? I am struck with admiration for the strength of character of the municipal authorities of New York who have preserved granite rocks and trees in the centre of Manhattan, a park more than four and a half million square yards [just over four million square metres] in area.

When the Cathedrals were White
Translated by Francis E. Hyslop, 1947

Roots, fossils, bones, pebbles or flints can all be 'objects provoking a poetic reaction', the source of inspiration for painting and sculpture, as Le Corbusier describes in his Entretien avec les étudiants des écoles d'architecture *(1943).*

Nature can make its own miraculous contribution. Take for example what I call 'objects provoking a poetic reaction': because of their shape and size, their materials and their durability, they are capable of featuring in a domestic setting. It might be a pebble worn smooth by the ocean, or a broken brick with its corners rounded off by the waters of a lake or river; bones, fossils, the roots of trees, seaweeds, often partly fossilized. Whole shells as smooth as porcelain or moulded into the shape of Greek or Indian sculptures; broken shells revealing their amazing helicoid structure; seeds, flints, crystals, bits of stone or wood – an infinite variety of evidence of the language of nature, caressed by your hands, scrutinized by your eye, evocative companions…. We have them to thank for the friendly relations that exist between people and Nature. At one time I used them as

subjects for my paintings and murals. They represent different characteristics: the male and female, vegetable and mineral, the bud and the fruit…every nuance…every form…. We men and women are positioned here in the midst of life, reacting to life with our honed and toughened sensibilities, furnishing our own minds, being effective, or at least not being passive, inattentive to life: operating and, as a result, participating. Participating, gauging, appreciating. Happy to be in direct contact with Nature which communicates such strength, purity, unity and diversity. I should like to see you drawing this succession of shapes and forms, this evidence of the organic, these eloquent spokesmen with their size and shape governed by natural, cosmic rules and regulations: pebbles, crystals, plants or the rudiments of plants. Nature's lessons extend to the clouds and rain, to erosion in the midst of geological reality, to those decisive sights seen from the aeroplane…. Nature, our shelter, is the battlefield for the eternally warring elements. These lessons would replace the dreary study of classical plaster casts that has dulled our appreciation of the Greeks and Romans, just as learning catechism tarnished the brilliance of the Scriptures. We shy away from very positive colours as we shy away from certain building styles.

Progress. *When the Cathedrals were White.*

Le Corbusier hopes that, imbued with the 'new spirit', architects will be freed from models inherited from the past, and will produce a new type of architecture and new cities, devised to make men happy and built to a human scale.

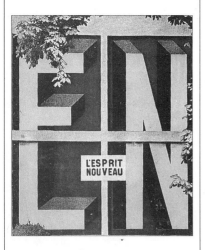

The *Esprit nouveau* embraced new graphic design.

When the Cathedrals were White, with its provocative title, contrasts the audacity of the men who built the 'holy skyscrapers' that dominated the medieval townscape with the timorous nature of 20th-century architects.

I should like to bring to an examination of conscience and to repentance those who, with all the ferocity of their hatred, of their fright, of their poverty of spirit, of their lack of vitality, concern themselves with a fatal stubbornness in the destruction and hindrance of whatever is most beautiful in this country – France – and in this period: the invention, the courage and the creative genius occupied especially with questions of building – with those things in which reason and poetry co-exist, in which wisdom and enterprise join hands.

When the cathedrals were white, Europe had organized the crafts under the imperative impulse of a quite new, marvellous and exceedingly daring technique, the use of which led to unexpected systems of forms – in fact to forms whose spirit disdained the legacy of a thousand years of tradition, not hesitating to thrust civilization towards an unknown adventure. An international language reigned wherever the white race was, favouring the exchange of ideas and the transfer of culture. An international style had spread from the West to the East and from the North to the South – a style which carried with it the passionate stream of spiritual delights: love of art, disinterestedness, joy of living in creating.

The cathedrals were white because they were new. The cities were new; they were constructed all at once, in an orderly way, regular, geometric, in accordance with plans. The freshly cut stone of France was dazzling in its whiteness, as the Acropolis in Athens had been white and dazzling, as the Pyramids of Egypt had gleamed with polished granite. Above all the cities and towns encircled by new walls, the skyscrapers of God dominated the countryside. They had made them as high as possible, extraordinarily high. It may seem a disproportion in the ensemble. Not at all, it was an act of optimism, a gesture of courage, a sign of pride, a proof of mastery! In addressing themselves to God men did not sign their own abdication.

The new world was beginning. White, limpid, joyous, clean, clear and without hesitations, the new world was opening up like a flower among the ruins. They left behind them all recognized ways of doing things; they turned their backs on all that. In a hundred years the marvel was accomplished and Europe was changed.

The cathedrals were white…. I wish to show only the great similarity between that past time and the present day. The cathedrals of our own time have not yet been built. The cathedrals belong to other people – to the dead – they are black with grime and worn by centuries. Everything is blackened by soot and eaten away by wear and tear: institutions, education, cities, farms, our lives, our hearts, our thoughts. Nevertheless, everything is potentially new, fresh, in the process of birth. Eyes which are turned away from dead things already are looking forward. The wind is changing; the winter wind gives way to the wind of spring; the sky is dark with clouds; they are being borne away.

Eyes that see, persons with knowledge, they must be allowed to construct the new world. When the first white cathedrals of the new world are standing, it will be seen and known that they are something true, that something has really begun. With what enthusiasm, what fervour, what relief, the about-face will be made! The proof will be there. Fearful, the world first wants proof.

The proof? The proof, in this country, is that the cathedrals were once white….

There is no crisis in life.

There is crisis only in a corporation: that of the makers of art.

The plastic artists of the world are everywhere in the midst of an intense, multiple, unlimited production. Every day, every hour, the Earth sees splendours surging up which are truths and *present-day* beauty. Ephemeral perhaps! Tomorrow, new truths and new beauties bloom. The day after tomorrow, etc….

Thus life is replenished, full. Life is beautiful! We do not have – do we? – any intention or claim to fix the destiny of the eternal *things of the future*? Everything, at every hour, is only the work of the present moment.

The present moment is creative, creating with an unheard of intensity.

A great epoch has begun.

A new epoch.

Already manifest in innumerable individual and collective works, forming part of the totality of contemporary production; surging from studios, mills, factories, from the minds of engineers, of artists – objects, laws, projects, thoughts – machine civilization breaks forth.

New times! It was in every way similar, once, seven centuries ago, when a new world was being born, when the cathedrals were white!

When the Cathedrals were White
Translated by Francis E. Hyslop, 1947

In Vers une architecture, *translated as* Towards a New Architecture, *Le Corbusier proclaims his admiration for machinery, steamships and aeroplanes.*

Architects live and move within the narrow limits of academic acquirements and in ignorance of new ways of building, and they are quite willing that their conceptions should remain at doves kissing one another. But our daring and masterly constructors of steamships produce palaces in comparison with which cathedrals are tiny things, and they throw them on to the sea!

Architecture is stifled by custom....

If we forget for a moment that a steamship is a machine for transport and look at it with a fresh eye, we shall feel that we are facing an important manifestation of temerity, of discipline, of harmony, of a beauty that is calm, vital and strong.

A seriously-minded architect, looking at it as an architect (i.e. a creator of organisms), will find in a steamship his freedom from an age-long but contemptible enslavement to the past.

He will prefer respect for the forces of nature to a lazy respect for tradition; to the narrowness of commonplace conceptions he will prefer the majesty of solutions which spring from a problem that has been clearly stated – solutions needed by this age of mighty effort which has taken so gigantic a step forward. The house of the earth-man is the expression of a circumscribed world. The steamship is the first stage in the realization of a world organized according to the new spirit....

There is one profession and one only, namely architecture, in which progress is not considered necessary, where laziness is enthroned, and in which the reference is always to yesterday.

Everywhere else, taking thought for the morrow is almost a fever and brings its inevitable solution: if a man does not move forward he becomes bankrupt.

But in architecture no one ever becomes bankrupt. A privileged profession, alas!...

Let us look at things from the point of view of architecture, but in the state of mind of the inventor of aeroplanes.

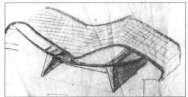

The lesson of the aeroplane is not primarily in the forms it has created, and above all we must learn to see in an aeroplane not a bird or a dragon-fly, but a machine for flying; the lesson of the aeroplane lies in the logic which governed the enunciation of the problem and which led to its successful realization. When a problem is properly stated, in our epoch, it inevitably finds its solution.

The problem of the house has not yet been stated.

Towards a New Architecture
Translated by Frederick Etchells, 1927

Le Corbusier's new world extended from furniture (left, sketch of a chaise longue) to cities (below, the 1925 Plan Voisin of Paris).

In L'Art décoratif d'aujourd'hui *Le Corbusier voices his admiration for the beauty of the machine, a mathematically planned expression of truth and accuracy.*

The miracle of the machine thus lies in having created harmonious organs, that is to say, organs of a harmony that approaches perfection to the extent that they have been purified by experience and invention.

All human endeavours are put to the proof sooner or later, that is to say, once they have registered on the human spirit, on the human heart, on the human conscience; the test may be delayed in matters that affect our emotions; the years pass, men die falsely celebrated or unjustly disparaged; rehabilitation comes late, and so does deserved demotion. In the present confusion of the arts it would be good to shorten this process, protracted and delayed by the innumerable outgrowths sown by the centuries. With the machine the test is immediate; *this one runs, that one does not*! The relationship between cause and effect is direct.

Broadly, one can say that every machine that runs is a present truth. It is a viable entity, it is a *clear organism*. I believe that it is towards this clarity, this healthy vitality that our sympathies are directed; paternal feelings: a being has been created that is alive.

But other factors add to these obscure, deep, true feelings. The machine is calculation; calculation is a creative human system that complements our natural abilities, explaining to our eyes the universe of which we are dimly aware by means of its exact analyses, and the nature that we see around us by means of its tangible demonstrations of order in life. The graphical expression of calculation is geometry; calculation is brought into action on the basis of geometry, the means [of] which *is our own*, which is dear to us, and by which alone we can measure events and objects. The machine is all geometry. Geometry is our greatest creation and we are enthralled by it. The direct mechanism of sight and touch, of the senses, is thus in play. The machine is certainly a marvellous field for experiment in the physiology of the senses, altogether richer and more *ordered* than statuary.

The Decorative Art of Today
Translated by James I. Dunnett, 1987

As early as 1914 Le Corbusier was promoting the idea of mass-produced houses built using industrially produced modular elements; he outlines the principle in Towards a New Architecture.

A great epoch has begun.

There exists a new spirit.

Industry, overwhelming us like a flood which rolls on towards its destined end, has furnished us with new tools adapted to this new epoch, animated by the new spirit.

Economic law unavoidably governs our acts and our thoughts.

The problem of the house is a problem of the epoch. The equilibrium of society today depends upon it. Architecture has for its first duty, in this period of renewal, that of bringing about a revision of values, a revision of the constituent elements of the house.

Mass-production is based on analysis and experiment.

Industry on the grand scale must occupy itself with building and establish the elements of the house on a mass-production basis.

We must create the mass-production spirit.

The spirit of constructing mass-production houses.

The spirit of living in mass-production houses.

The spirit of conceiving mass-production houses.

If we eliminate from our hearts and minds all dead concepts in regard to the houses and look at the question from a critical and objective point of view, we shall arrive at the 'House Machine', the mass-production house, healthy (and morally so too) and beautiful in the same way that the working tools and instruments which accompany our existence are beautiful.

Beautiful also with all the animation that the artist's sensibility can add to severe and pure functioning elements....

Now, it was necessary to start from the very beginning; nothing being ready for the realization of such an immense programme. *The right state of mind does not exist....*

The reason is that the various objects have not been standardized. As the necessary state of mind does not exist, attention has never been given to the serious study of the various units, and still less to that of the construction itself; the mass-production state of mind is hateful to architects and to the ordinary man (by infection and persuasion).

The prime consequences of the industrial evolution in 'building' show themselves in this first stage; the replacing of natural materials by artificial ones, of heterogenous and doubtful materials by homogenous and artificial ones (tried and proved in the laboratory) and by products of fixed composition. Natural materials, which are infinitely variable in composition, must be replaced by fixed ones.

As early as 1914, the Dom-ino principle was intended for mass-production.

On the other hand the laws of economics demand their rights: steel girders and, more recently, reinforced concrete, are pure manifestations of calculation, using the material of which they are composed in its entirety and absolutely exactly....

One thing leads to another, and as so many cannons, aeroplanes, lorries and wagons had been made in factories, someone asked the question: 'Why not make houses?' There you have a state of mind really belonging to our epoch. Nothing is ready, but everything can be done. In the next twenty years, big industry will have co-ordinated its standardized materials, comparable with those of metallurgy; technical achievement will have carried heating and lighting and methods of rational construction far beyond anything we are acquainted with.... Dwellings, urban and suburban, will be enormous and square-built and no longer a dismal congeries; they will incorporate the principle of mass-production and of large-scale industrialization. It is even possible that building 'to measure' will cease. An inevitable social evolution will have transformed the relationship between tenant and landlord, will have modified the current conception of the dwelling-house, and our towns will be ordered instead of being chaotic. A house will no longer be this solidly built thing which sets out to defy time and decay, and which is an expensive luxury by which wealth can be shown; it will be a tool as the motor-car is becoming a tool. The house will no longer be an archaic entity, heavily rooted in the soil by deep foundations, built 'firm and strong', the object of the devotion on which the cult of the family and the race has so long been concentrated.

Towards a New Architecture
Translated by Frederick Etchells, 1927

Architecture is made to arouse emotion

Unlike most of his fellow-architects, Le Corbusier was a prolific writer. He needed to write in order to give his ideas an airing, to analyse or reconsider thoughts already expressed on the drawing board or the building site. Though his architectural expression was subject to constant renewal, he remained faithful to a set of key ideas throughout his career.

In Towards a New Architecture *Le Corbusier contends that besides being construction, architecture is made to arouse emotion.*

You employ stone, wood and concrete, and with these materials you build houses and palaces; that is construction. Ingenuity is at work.

But suddenly you touch my heart, you do me good, I am happy and I say: 'This is beautiful'. That is Architecture. Art enters in.

My house is practical. I thank you, as I might thank Railway engineers or the Telephone service. You have not touched my heart.

But suppose that walls rise towards heaven in such a way that I am moved. I perceive your intentions. Your mood has been gentle, brutal, charming or noble. The stones you have erected tell me so. You fix me to the place and my eyes regard it. They behold something which expresses a thought. A thought which reveals itself without word or sound, but solely by means of shapes which stand in a certain relationship to one another. These shapes are such that they are clearly revealed in light. The relationships between them have not necessarily any reference to what is practical or descriptive. They are a mathematical creation of your mind. They are the language of Architecture. By the use of inert materials and *starting from* conditions more or less utilitarian, you have established certain relationships which have aroused my emotions. That is Architecture.

Towards a New Architecture
Translated by Frederick Etchells, 1927

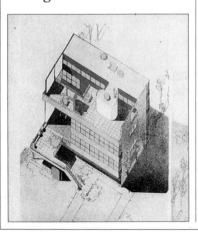

The Villa Stein, like all Purist villas, provided 'architectural promenades'.

In L'Almanach d'architecture moderne *(1925), Le Corbusier returns to the argument about construction and architecture: a house is a machine for living, but constructed for human beings.*

A house has two functions. First, it is a *machine for living*, which means a machine designed to make our daily work as rapid and as simple as possible, and to look after our bodily needs attentively, providing comfort. It also provides surroundings where meditation can take place, and a place in which beauty brings the repose of spirit which is so indispensable. Of course I am not suggesting that art is everyone's cup of tea, but simply that for certain people it is important that their house provides them with a feeling of beauty. The engineer deals with the practical aspects of a dwelling, but it is the architect who is responsible for providing an atmosphere conducive to meditation, a sense of beauty, and orderliness as a prop to beauty. Engineers' work on one side, architects' on the other.

A house is the direct product of the phenomenon of anthropocentrism: everything stems from and leads back to human beings. This is for the simple reason that the house is of interest only to oneself, but it is of more interest than anything else; the house mirrors our behaviour – it is the snail's shell. It must be made to measure.

It is essential therefore to relate everything to the human scale. This is the only solution, the only way of solving the present problem of architecture; there has to be a complete review of current values after a period which has, in effect, been the last wave of the Renaissance, the end of nearly six centuries of pre-machine age culture, a brilliant period now in ruins at the onset of the machine age, a period which, unlike our own, was dedicated to outward display, palaces for princes, churches for the popes.

Le Corbusier maintained that architecture should be viewed in motion, while walking. This idea was embodied in a number of his buildings, and he wrote about it in his Entretien avec les étudiants des écoles d'architecture (1943).

Architecture has to be *walked, travelled* and is not (as is sometimes taught) a graphic illusion organized around a central point, supposedly the figure of a man, but an imaginary man with composite eyes (like a fly) and radial vision. Such a man does not exist, and the confusion this caused was responsible for the shipwreck of architecture after the classical period. Our man is provided with two eyes, approximately 1m 60 [over 5 feet] above the ground and facing forwards. This is a biological truth and should be enough to discredit all those plans centring around an erroneous central hub. Armed with his two eyes, and facing forwards, our man walks about, going about his business, taking notice of the succession of architectural events as they unfurl one by one. He experiences a succession of pleasant flutters of excitement....

The terms 'life' and 'death' have been applied to the exterior perambulation of a building, the life and death of architectural sensation, the life and death of emotion. How much more appropriate would this concept be if applied to *interior* perambulation. A living person is sometimes crudely referred to as a digestive tube. We could call architecture (equally crudely) interior perambulation, and not only for functional reasons...but particularly for emotional reasons: the appearance of the building from different angles, the symphony it plays, in fact – which can only be grasped as our feet carry us along, shifting us through the building. We gaze on the walls and perspectives, the surprises behind the doors that lead to new space, the succession of shadow, half-shadow and light provided by the sun shining through openings or windows; views of urban or rural landscapes in the distance, beyond carefully designed surroundings of the immediate environment. The quality of the interior perambulation represents the work's biological strength. The organization of the building as it relates to its purpose. Good architecture can be 'walked' or 'travelled' inside as well as out. This is living architecture. Bad architecture is fixed, stuck, frozen, coagulated around a spurious central hub; it bears no relation to the laws of the human race.

Le Corbusier regarded the plan as fundamental and architecture as its outcome, but the façade needs also to be organized with great precision, using regulating lines. The site around a building should be considered as part of the overall plan as well. These three ideas are set out in Towards a New Architecture.

The plan

To make a plan is to determine and fix ideas. It is to have had ideas.

It is so to order these ideas that they become intelligible, capable of execution and communicable. It is essential therefore to exhibit a precise intention, and to have had ideas in order to be able to furnish oneself with an intention. A plan is to some extent a summary like an analytical contents table. In a form so condensed that it seems as clear as crystal and like a geometrical figure, it contains an enormous quantity of ideas and the impulse of an intention.

In a great public institution, the Ecole des Beaux-Arts, the principles of good planning have been studied, and then as time has gone by, dogmas have been established, and recipes and tricks. A method of teaching useful enough at the beginning has become a dangerous practice. To represent the inner meaning certain hallowed external signs and aspects have been fixed. The plan, which is really a cluster of ideas and of the intention essential to this cluster of ideas, has become a piece of paper on which black marks for walls and lines for axes play at a sort of mosaic on a decorative panel making graphic representations of star-patterns, creating an optical illusion. The most beautiful star becomes the Grand Prix de Rome. Now, the plan is the generator, 'the plan is the determination of everything; it is an austere abstraction, an algebrization, and cold of aspect'. It is a plan of battle. The battle follows and that is the great moment. The battle is composed of the impact of masses in space and the *morale* of the army is the cluster of predetermined ideas and the driving purpose. Without a good plan nothing exists, all is frail and cannot endure, all is poor even under the clutter of the richest decoration.

From the very start the plan implies the methods of construction to be used; the architect is above all an engineer. But let us keep strictly to architecture, this thing which endures through the ages. Placing myself entirely at this one angle of vision I commence by drawing attention to this vital fact: a plan proceeds *from within to without*, for a house or a palace is an organism comparable to a living being. I shall speak of the architectural *elements* of the interior. I shall pass on to *arrangement*. In considering the effect of buildings in relation to a site, I shall show that here too the *exterior* is always an *interior*.

The regulating lines

A regulating line is an assurance against capriciousness: it is a means of verification which can ratify all work created in a fervour, the schoolboy's rule of nine, the Q.E.D. of the mathematician.

The regulating line is a satisfaction of a spiritual order which leads to the pursuit of ingenious and harmonious relations. It confers on the work the quality of rhythm.

The regulating line brings in this tangible form of mathematics which gives the reassuring perception of order. The choice of a regulating line fixes the

•Regulating lines• on the façade of Notre-Dame de Paris, by Jeanneret.

fundamental geometry of the work; it fixes therefore one of the 'fundamental characters'. The choice of the regulating line is one of the decisive moments of inspiration, it is one of the vital operations of architecture....

The exterior is always an interior

When, at the schools, they draw axes in the shape of a star, they imagine that the spectator arriving in front of a building is aware of it alone, and that his eye must infallibly follow and remain exclusively fixed on the centre of gravity determined by these axes. The human eye, in its investigations, is always on the move and the beholder himself is always turning right and left, and shifting about. He is interested in everything and is attracted towards the centre of gravity of the whole site. At once the problem spreads to the surroundings. The houses near by, the distant or neighbouring mountains, the horizon low or high, make formidable masses which exercise the force of their cubic volume. This cubic volume, as it appears and as it really is, is instantly gauged and anticipated by the intelligence. This sensation of cubic volume is immediate and fundamental; your building may cube 100,000 cubic yards, but what lies around it may cube millions of cubic yards, and that is what tells. Then there comes the sensation of density: a tree or a hill is less powerful and of a feebler density than a geometrical disposition of forms. Marble is denser, both to the eye and to the mind, than is wood, and so forth. Always you have gradation.

To sum up, in architectural ensembles, the elements of the site itself come into play by virtue of their cubic volume, their density and the quality of the material of which they are composed, bringing sensations which are

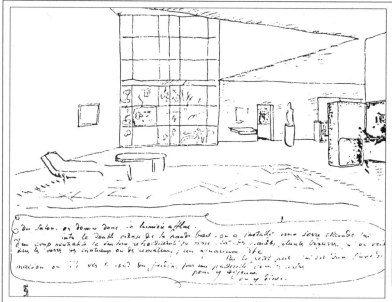

The living room 'has a magnificent view' of the trees (letter to Madame Meyer).

very definite and very varied (wood, marble, a tree, grass, blue horizons, near or distant sea, sky). The elements of the site rise up like walls panoplied in the power of their cubic co-efficient, stratification, material, etc., like the walls of a room. Walls in relation to light, light and shade, sadness, gaiety or serenity, etc. Our compositions must be formed of these elements.

Towards a New Architecture
Translated by Frederick Etchells, 1927

The act of creation is especially difficult for the architect because of the precision it requires. In a letter written to a client, Madame Meyer, in 1925, Le Corbusier explains that 'simple does not mean easy'.

Our dream was to make you a house that was as sleek and as serene as a well-proportioned casket, without the lumps and bumps added to create a bogus picturesque effect – these look so bad in daylight and serve only to add to the surrounding chaos. We disagree with the fashion, current here and abroad, for complicated, jumbled houses. We think that the sum is more important than the parts. Please do not think that the sleekness is the effect of laziness: on the contrary, it is the outcome of intense and prolonged deliberation. Simple does not mean easy. In fact this house would have had great dignity, standing against the trees…. The front door would be on the side, not in the centre. Would this incur the Academy's wrath?…

The entrance hall is large and flooded with light…the coat cupboard and toilet are concealed. The hall is directly accessible from the domestic areas. If you go upstairs you will find the living room, above the shade of the trees and giving a magnificent view of the tree-tops. With plenty of sky.... If domestics are comfortably accommodated, the house will be kept sparkling. No attics, because the roof will house a garden, a solarium and a swimming pool. From the living room you overlook the greenery and light pours in. The big window is double glazed, with a conservatory between the two layers which neutralizes the chill of the glass surface; this contains interesting plants such as might be found in the greenhouses of country houses or horticulturalists; an aquarium, etc. The small outside door in the centre of the house leads via a raised gangway to the end of the garden, where you can have lunch or dinner under the trees....

This floor consists of just one room, drawing room, dining room, etc. library. Oh yes! The services! Right in the middle. Of course! So that the pipe can be useful. It's made of cork bricks which insulate it like a telephone booth or a thermos. Strange idea? Not really...it's natural. The services go right through the house from top to bottom like an artery. Where better to locate them? The back walls and the walls of the service cylinder could be covered. You can see the boudoir with its built-in cupboards.

This boudoir looks out over trees and the summer dining area. If you want to put on plays you could use the boudoir as a dressing room. Two staircases lead down to the stage in front of the big window.... The service pipe goes up to the door beside the swimming pool and behind them both is a little area where you can have breakfast.

From the boudoir we have gone up to the roof, which has neither tiles nor slates. It houses a solarium and a swimming pool with grass growing between the paving. The sky is overhead. The surrounding walls prevent your being seen. In the evening all you see is stars and the dark outline of the trees in the Folie Saint-James. Sliding screens ensure complete protection.... This garden is not typically French; it's a wild garden.... The kitchens etc. receive sunshine round the clock.... This plan was not produced by some hurried office draughtsman, between two telephone calls. The solutions for a classic site like this were considered, mulled over, at great length, in complete tranquillity.

Such ideas...such architectural themes, possessing as they do a kind of poetry, are subject to the most rigorous constructional regulations. Twelve concrete columns, evenly spaced, easily support the floor. Inside the concrete box thus created the design is so simple that one is tempted to regard it as simple-minded.... We have been accustomed for years to see plans that are so complicated that they look like people wearing their viscera on the outside. We prefer viscera to be inside, organized and tidy, and just a sleek shape outside. Not so easy! The hardest thing about architecture is getting things into line. In order to extract its poetry, this kind of architecture requires meticulous organization. Once it's built everything looks simple and straightforward. And that's a good sign. But when the first sketches for plans are drawn up it's all confusion.

If the structure and layout are extremely simple the contractor can be a little less demanding. That makes a difference. It makes a huge difference, and stringent economy is only acceptable once the solution has begun to emerge. Praise of architects! Complacency like that has to raise a smile. One has to laugh occasionally....

Modern decorative art is not decorated

In everything he did, Le Corbusier combined the aesthetic with the moral dimension. Through Purism, with its precision and order, he sought satisfaction for the mind and soul, as well as the eye. He pushed the double strand, moral and aesthetic, to extraordinary lengths.

The decorative art of today

As Le Corbusier explains in L'Art décoratif d'aujourd'hui, *art is necessary to people, but 'art' is not useless decoration.*

The decorative art of today! Am I plunging into a paradox? – a paradox that is only apparent. To include under this rubric everything that is free from decoration, whilst making due apology for what is simply banal, indifferent or void of *artistic intention*, to invite the eye and the spirit to take pleasure in the company of such things and perhaps to rebel against the flourish, the stain, the distracting din of colours and ornaments, to dismiss a whole mass of artefacts, some of which are not without merit, to pass over an activity that has sometimes been disinterested, sometimes idealistic, to disdain the work of so many schools, so many masters, so

The 'equipment' of an apartment. Detail of the dividing wall between the living room and bedroom, constructed from modular shelving units. Show at the Salon d'Automne, Paris, in 1929.

many pupils, and to think thus of them: 'they are as disagreeable as mosquitoes'; and thence to arrive at this impasse: *modern decorative art is not decorated.* Have we not the right? A moment's thought will confirm it. The paradox lies not in reality, but in the words. Why do the objects that concern us here have to be called *decorative art*? This is the paradox: why should chairs, bottles, baskets, shoes, which are all objects of utility, all *tools*, be called *decorative art*? The paradox of making art out of tools. Let's be clear. I mean, the paradox of making *decorative* art out of tools.

To make art out of tools is fair enough, if we hold with Larousse's definition, which is that ART is the *application of knowledge to the realization of an idea.* Then yes. We are indeed committed to apply all our knowledge to the perfect creation of a tool: know-how, skill, efficiency, economy, precision, the sum

of knowledge. A good tool, an excellent tool, the very best tool. This is the world of *manufacture*, of industry; we are looking for a standard and our concerns are far from the personal, the arbitrary, the fantastic, the eccentric; our interest is in the norm, and we are creating type-objects.

So the paradox certainly lies in the terminology.

But we are told that decoration is necessary to our existence. Let us correct that: art is necessary to us; that is to say, a disinterested passion that exalts us. Decoration: baubles, charming entertainment for a savage. (And I do not deny that it is an excellent thing to keep an element of the savage alive in us – a small one.) But in the 20th century our powers of judgement have developed greatly and we have raised our level of consciousness. Our spiritual needs are different, and higher worlds than those of decoration offer us commensurate experience. It seems justified to affirm: *the more cultivated a people becomes, the more decoration disappears.* (Surely it was Loos who put it so neatly.)

So to see things clearly, it is sufficient to separate the satisfaction of disinterested emotion from that of utilitarian need. Utilitarian needs call for tools brought in *every respect* to that degree of perfection seen in industry. This then is the magnificent programme for decorative art (decidedly, an inappropriate term!)....

Previously, decorative objects were rare and costly. Today they are commonplace and cheap. Previously, plain objects were commonplace and cheap; today they are rare and expensive: previously, decorative objects were items for special display; the plate which the peasant family hung on the wall and the embroidered waistcoat for holidays; grist for the propaganda of princes. Today decorative objects flood the shelves of the Department Stores; they sell cheaply to shop-girls. If they sell cheaply, it is because they are badly made and because decoration hides faults in their manufacture and the poor quality of their materials: decoration is disguise. It pays the manufacturer to employ a decorator to disguise the faults in his products, to conceal the poor quality of their materials and to distract the eye from their blemishes by offering it the spiced morsels of glowing gold-plate and strident symphonies. Trash is always abundantly decorated; the luxury object is well-made, neat and clean, pure and healthy, and its bareness reveals the quality of its manufacture. It is to industry that we owe this reversal in the state of affairs: a cast-iron stove overflowing with decoration cost less than a plain one; amidst the surging leaf patterns flaws in the casting cannot be seen. And the same applies generally....

Day after day, on the other hand, we notice among the products of industry articles of perfect convenience and utility, that soothe our spirits with the luxury afforded by the elegance of their conception, the purity of their execution and the efficiency of their operation. They are so well thought out that we feel them to be harmonious, and this harmony is sufficient for our gratification....

This rational perfection and precise formulation in each does not constitute sufficient common ground between them to allow the recognition of a *style*!

During these last years we have witnessed the successive stages of a development: with metallic construction, the *separation of decoration from structure*. Then the fashion for

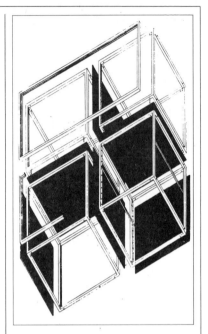

expressing the construction, the sign of a new construction. Then the ecstasy before *nature*, showing a desire to rediscover (by how circuitous a path!) the laws of *the organic*. Then the craze for the *simple*, the first contact with the truths of the machine leading us back to good sense, and the instinctive manifestation of an aesthetic for our era.

The Decorative Art of Today
Translated by James I. Dunnett, 1987

A coat of whitewash

If some Solon imposed these two laws on our enthusiasm:

THE LAW OF RIPOLIN
A COAT OF WHITEWASH

M odular units (opposite) compose a built-in storage space separating kitchen and living room (above).

we would perform a moral act: *to love purity*!
we would improve our condition: *to have the power of judgment*!

An act which leads to the joy of life: the pursuit of perfection....

On white ripolin walls these accretions of dead things from the past would be intolerable: they would leave a mark. Whereas the marks do not show on the medley of our damasks and patterned wall-papers....

If the house is all white, the outline of things stands out from it without any possibility of mistake; their volume shows clearly; their colour is distinct. The white of whitewash is absolute, everything stands out from it and is recorded absolutely, black on white; it is honest and dependable.

Put on it anything dishonest or in bad taste – it hits you in the eye. It is rather like an X-ray of beauty. It is a court of assize in permanent session. It is the eye of truth.

Whitewash is extremely moral. Suppose there were a decree requiring

all rooms in Paris to be given a coat of whitewash. I maintain that that would be a police task of real stature and a manifestation of high morality, the sign of a great people.

Whitewash is the wealth of the poor and of the rich – of everybody, just as bread, milk and water are the wealth of the slave and of the king.

The Decorative Art of Today
Translated by James I. Dunnett, 1987

In Précisions sur un état présent de l'architecture et de l'urbanisme *(1930), Le Corbusier suggests that furniture is just a collection of tools, designed (like any other modern means of production) to meet our many needs.*

What then is furniture?
Furniture is:
– tables for working at and eating.
– chairs for eating and working.
– armchairs of different shapes for resting in different ways.
– and *cabinets* for storing the objects we use.
Furniture is tools,
And also servants.
Furniture serves our needs.

Our needs are daily, regular, always the same; yes, always the same.

Our furniture corresponds to *constant, daily, regular functions.*

All people have the same needs, at the same hours, every day, all their lives.

The tools corresponding to these functions are easy to define. And progress, bringing us new techniques, steel tubing, folded sheet metal, welding, gives us the means to carry them out infinitely more perfectly and more efficiently than in the past.

House interiors will no longer resemble the Louis XIV style.

There is the adventure.

The synthesis of all the arts

Le Corbusier viewed all architecture as a dialogue between buildings and their surroundings. 'The temples on the Acropolis have made the desolate countryside around them part of the composition.' Other examples of the visual arts – architecture, sculpture, painting – have a similar dialogue with their architectural setting.

Indescribable space

The first act of a living creature, man or animal, plant or cloud, is to take possession of its space; this basic gesture is an expression of equilibrium and of continuity. The first proof of existence is to occupy space.

A flower, plant, tree or mountain stands in an environment. If one of them attracts attention because of its comforting presence, or its dignity, this is because it appears materially detached, yet provokes echoes all around it. We stop, aware of these natural affinities; and we stare, moved by the way such synchronization affects such a large area. And we begin to assess what we are staring at so fixedly.

Architecture, sculpture and painting are dependant on space in specific ways, each needing to manage its own space

Le Corbusier's studio in the Molitor flats.

appropriately. Basically, what I shall be demonstrating here is that aesthetic emotion is a function of space.

The action of a work of art (architecture, sculpture or painting) on its surroundings: waves, cries and clamour (the Parthenon on the Acropolis in Athens) flashes like the flashes of an explosion; the site, whether nearby or far away, is jolted, moved, mastered, caressed. This is the reaction of the whole environment: the walls of the room, its dimensions, the square with its façades of varying weights, stretches of landscape, slopes and the bare horizons of the plain, the jagged horizon with mountains, the weight of the atmosphere is concentrated on this place with its work of art (a manifestation of our will) and fixes its depths and its heights, its hard and soft parts, its violence and its gentleness. A phenomenon of synchronization occurs which is as precise as anything in mathematics, a true example of plastic acoustics; it might thus be permissible to class this phenomenon amongst the most subtle of its kind. It can bring happiness (music) or oppression (din or racket).

Without wishing to seem pretentious, I want to make a declaration relating to the 'magnification' of space by artists of my generation in the first heady rapture of Cubism, in about 1910. They spoke of the *fourth dimension*, whether with intuition or clairvoyance it does not matter. A life devoted to art, in particular to the search for harmony, and practice in the three arts – architecture, sculpture, painting has permitted me to observe the phenomenon myself....

When the long and difficult process of detachment from times past is accomplished, an important truth is revealed, namely that the synthesis of all the major arts (architecture, sculpture, painting) is today possible, under the dominion of space. Perspectives in the Italian style can alter nothing; something quite different has come to pass. This something has been named the fourth dimension, and why not? Since it is subjective, undeniable yet indefinable, and not Euclidean; this discovery will shatter quite a number of superficial, modish assertions such as that painting should not make a hole in the wall, sculpture must be fixed to the ground....

In my belief no work of art is without its unfathomable depths; each slips its moorings. Art is the spatial science *par excellence.* Picasso, Braque, Léger, Brancusi, Laurens, Giacometti, Lipchitz, painters or sculptors, have all devoted their lives to the same goal.

Now we understand just how successful a marriage between art and architecture can be: a partnership as strongly constructed as a Cézanne.

The air is full of intoxicating opportunities at the meeting of the major arts at the Golden Gate. By helping one another they will dispel the fog that envelops ideas and artists, leaving metope, pediment and tympanum in their rightful (and uncontested) positions. This alliance will be something else. Urbanism disposes, architecture creates, sculpture and painting communicate the well-chosen words that are the reason for their existence.

It is interesting to observe how events are on the move, and how people, stupefied, watch them pass, forgetting to catch the bus and reach the appointment in time.

The appointment is important nowadays, in a world that is renewing

Purist still-life, by Charles-Edouard Jeanneret (not then called Le Corbusier), published in *L'Esprit nouveau*.

itself so rapidly; society is disposing of the vestiges of early machinism and trying to settle into the second phase – to function, to feel, to rule.

'L'Espace indicible'
Architecture d'aujourd'hui, April 1946

Le Corbusier practised drawing all his life. In an essay, Dessins, written in 1965, he explains that his artistic activities, drawing, painting and sculpture, were the secret laboratory for his architecture.

Drawing is primarily a way of looking at things, of observing and discovering. To draw is to learn to see, to see things and people being born, developing, flourishing and dying. Drawing is

necessary because it internalizes what has been seen and inscribes it permanently in the memory.

To draw is to invent and to create. Invention occurs only after observation. The pencil explores for a while, and then goes into action, leading one well beyond what is in front of ones eyes. Biology is bound to make an appearance here, because all life is biology. You must delve into the heart of things, search, explore.

Drawing is a language, a science, a means of expression, a means of conveying ideas. By perpetuating the image of an object on the page, a drawing can be a document that contains all the elements needed to recall that object once the real one has disappeared.

A drawing can transmit an idea without any need for written or verbal explanation. Drawing helps ideas to crystallize and develop. For the artist, drawing is the only way of trying things out unrestrainedly – matters of taste, ways of expressing beauty or emotion. For the artist, drawing is his way of seeing solutions, observing, classifying; it is his way of using the things he wishes to observe – by first understanding and then translating and reproducing them.

Drawing can do without art. It need have nothing to do with it. However, art cannot exist without drawing.

Drawing is also a game. I have been told that the secret of wisdom is to know how to take time off. I agree. I'm always taking time off. Playing all day – cards, rugby, Indians, soldiers: children and men take these things really seriously. So do I: I've been drawing all my life. Landscapes, architecture, bottles and glasses, odds and ends, shells, stones, bones, pebbles, little female figures, beasts, these are the stages, the keys....

In art, the theme can be or can remain secret, or may only be revealed to the person who discovered that particular trail, or any trail...his own or the artist's. His own is acceptable. Everything is relative (human perception is a function of the individual).

One evening, after dinner, at my summer cabin at Cap-Martin by the Mediterranean, I was watching Vincent [a friend] playing the accordion for an elegant lady. Behind them was a balustrade, then the sea and the wonderful rocks. And the moon, too. In short, a mouthwatering scenario. A theme, this theme, the favourable timing, the moment when chords resolve etc., etc. All very fine. But it's dangerous, and anti-art. It should in fact be concealed behind or beneath the outcome. The outcome was to have been to play chords and to resolve them. But you are not required to do that. Don't shout it from the rooftops or put on an identity tag. Keep quiet. Work. Produce your piece (your painting). We are speaking to the painter....

At the age of seventy-seven, and by now an architect of some repute, I am required to explain how, with little formal training, I have managed to create a modern architectural sentiment. Although onlookers may come to very random conclusions, every person knows himself to be driven by a set of circumstances that for one reason or another he may not wish to make public. In my case I started off in 1918, beginning with a formulation of principles; I set off, left foot first, in a direction of my own choosing at the age of thirty. The storm broke immediately. In 1923, with criticism raining down on me from all sides, and occupied mainly with my work as an architect and town planner, I deliberately ceased to exist publicly as a painter, although I did not cease to paint privately.

There followed thirty years of silence, from 1923 to 1953.

In 1948 I wrote: 'I think that if my work as an architect is seen in a favourable light (today I would change that and say: if my work as an architect and town planner has been seen in a favourable light), its enduring worth is due to this secret labour.'

The *Unité d'habitation* in Marseilles

The revolutionary design of the Unité d'habitation *in Marseilles (below), the problems encountered while it was being built, the prevarication of the administration and Le Corbusier's provocative statements fuelled a succession of heated arguments during the five years it took to complete the project from 1947 to 1952.*

The *pilotis* free the space underneath, and also give it shade.

In La Journée du bâtiment, *an architect suggests that members of his profession should decide whether they think that 'La Maison Radieuse' is a mistake or not.*

On the subject of 'La Maison radieuse'…. If Le Corbusier was making an architectural joke, as we sometimes do in the office – a revolving house, perhaps, or a house shaped like a mushroom or something like that – it would not be particularly surprising. I would take his side against my colleagues if that were the case because I'm all in favour of people with ideas… If it's a choice between batty ideas (which one might regret afterwards) and the conservatism of some of the 'mandarins', I'd give my vote to Le Corbusier. This would not stop me, however, turning to my colleague right away and saying to him: 'there are certain things that are just not done'. Not everything is feasible, and human nature cannot be transformed so lightly.

Far more serious, in my opinion, is that Le Corbusier, having given birth to a monster (in the view of many) has delivered the monster (if it is a monster) into public hands. The seriousness of this state of affairs is compounded because it proves that our crazy city has no safety valve…. Even more worrying is the fact that certain countries in Latin America consider Le Corbusier to be the most important living exponent of modern French architecture….

If we examine our consciences, it is clear that we are all responsible when one person makes an error. The architectural profession has its statutes and regulations nowadays; artistically it reflects our own mental anarchy. We should convene a committee of artists and people of good taste and sound judgment on things contemporary who would be able to decide, at national level, whether or not 'La Maison radieuse' should be considered a mistake.

R. Rouzeau
La Journée du bâtiment
25–6 January 1948

On the other hand, the magazine Arts *published a positive view of the architectural and social benefits of the* Unité d'habitation.

To make perspicaceous comments about this building project you must have seen it. An opportunity to visit the site was offered to a number of privileged people by the minister for reconstruction, who wished to give to this experience the importance it deserves. Le Corbusier's *Unité d'habitation* in Marseilles presents us with a whole range of new experiences: the construction, the shape, the different surface finishes, the handling of light, air conditioning, comfort....

The building is tall, but it does not resemble a great cliff. The façade, 135 metres [over 440 feet] long and 52 metres [170 feet] high, looks airy with its horizontal stripes. It soon becomes clear that the *pilotis* six metres [nearly 20 feet] high on which the building stands are as necessary to its appearance as the feet of certain pieces of furniture; they have both moral and aesthetic advantages, clearing the ground beneath the building and preventing pedestrians from having to confront it head on. The great ship seems airborne; the struts divide the view into separate pictures.

Major construction work on the *Unité d'habitation* is complete. However this reinforced concrete shell, named 'the bottle rack' by Le Corbusier (and there could be no more telling image)

will not be habitable for another year. Nearly four hundred homes will occupy the compartments, stacked like bottles in the immense framework.

Everyone who has seen the *Unité d'habitation* and who is broad-minded enough to admit that is possible to build without using classical columns, recognizes the project as an architectural triumph. And not only the architecture commands attention. The building offers its inhabitants a new lifestyle. Do go and see it.

S. Gille-Delafon
Arts, 9 December 1949

Le Parisien libéré *reports on the lawsuit instituted by the 'Société pour l'esthétique général de la France', under the presidency of M. Texier, a senior state councillor, to halt construction.*

In defence of France's aesthetic values, M. Texier, a senior state councillor, has attacked the 'Cité radieuse', into which citizens of Marseilles are now beginning to move.

The 'Cité radieuse' has already cost something in the region of 3 billion, and will probably require a minor additional payment by the firm run by M. Le Corbusier, its creator, of about 20 million.

This is the sum of the damages claimed by M. Henri Texier, president of the 'Société pour l'esthétique générale de la France'....

What is all this? Apparently M. Texier, a senior state councillor, no less, has had his quality of life compromised by the enormous building erected by M. Le Corbusier in Boulevard Michelet. The revolutionary way in which this group of dwellings has been designed – with its 321 apartments, its shops, swimming pool, sports ground and crèche, and its

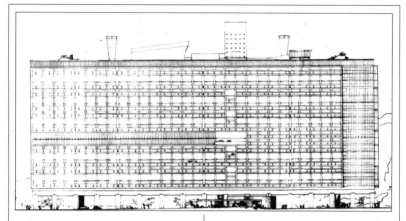

The *Unité d'habitation*, Marseilles.

eighteen internal 'streets' (each serving one storey) – is of less concern to him than the alien ugliness of this 'monster'.

The opinion of the first occupants, who proclaimed themselves delighted with things once they had got the hang of the open-plan kitchen/living room etc, was of no interest to the plaintiff: it was only M. Texier's aesthetic sensibility (and he is the self-appointed protector of the aesthetic sensibility of the whole country) that was injured.…

Lying behind M. Texier's artistic concerns are the more materialistic concerns of the architects whose plans were not chosen by M. Claudius-Petit and who, having been unable to prevent the building of the 'Cité radieuse', hope that at least this irritating precedent will not be repeated, especially in Nantes where a similar construction is already mooted.

Le Parisien libéré
25 August 1952

At the inauguration of the Unité *on 14 October 1952 Le Corbusier, standing on the roof terrace, was so overcome with emotion that he had the greatest difficulty in speaking.*

It gives me great honour, pleasure and pride to hand over to you this *Unité d'habitation de grandeur conforme* (to human scale), the first example in the world of a new type of human habitat, commissioned by the French government but free from any government control.… The result is right here…built, without regulations and in contravention of some of the more disastrous regulations; built for mankind, to a human scale, built using sturdy modern techniques; built to display the marvellous qualities of raw concrete; built to give the family (the building block of our society) access to the best of modern resources.

Eugène Claudius-Petit, minister for reconstruction and a keen supporter of Le Corbusier, proclaims his admiration for the architect's work. He was instrumental in procuring the Légion d'honneur for Le Corbusier.

I need not try to hide the emotion I feel; it follows on the heels of the emotion displayed by Le Corbusier to his friends and collaborators, his followers and helpers as we inaugurate, or, more precisely, acknowledge the presence of this *Unité d'habitation* that has caused such a stir and aroused such emotion; perhaps because so much has already been said about it, the *Unité* can leave nobody unmoved. Today we must put small-mindedness, meanness and misunderstanding to one side....

So what is the *Unité d'habitation*? These 320 dwellings are amongst the 249,000 built in France since the Liberation. This sets into its rightful context the volley of criticism about wasted resources and the personal delusions of the architect, Le Corbusier. These 320 dwellings are important, nevertheless. This is just one of a number of experimental apartment blocks built by the Government in the years following the Liberation, but it does seem as if it is the only one really worthy of the label 'experimental'. Everything is experimental: the concept of the block itself and of the individual dwellings, the extent to which each apartment is equipped and I might almost add the whole way of living in them. The most surprising thing of all perhaps is that the criticisms levelled at the block contradict the reality of the situation, blowing it out of all proportion. It's labelled a cavern, but it's much more like a monastic building. There's no noise, there never will be any, there will just be the type of cosy household that ideally suits the inhabitants of this city.

It has been labelled oddly promiscuous, yet never have children and parents been so separated. Little corners where children will get bored have been identified, but there's a terrace where children will be really happy, unlike their peers who have nothing but a stuffy, steamy kitchen to spend their long winter evenings in, and only a corner of pavement or the yard of a five- or six-storey house in which to play in spring or autumn – and often during the summer months as well, alas.

It has been labelled dark, yet the apartments are filled with light; it has been labelled uncomfortable – the apartments must be visited in summer, or sampled as homes even if just for a short time in summer when Marseilles swelters behind closed shutters trying to escape the sun's hottest rays; here the light can come right in and the atmosphere is comfortable because the angle of the building has been carefully considered, in the great tradition of the ancient Greeks.

Shortly after the inauguration, Eugène Claudius-Petit wrote to Le Corbusier's mother, by then ninety-two years old, to tell her about her son's extraordinary building.

We have just returned from Marseilles, from the only place that counts at the moment in Marseilles, your son's building.

If you had any doubts about the building, please be reassured. It's good. It's better than your friends were expecting. He had confidence in himself and he was right. Let his detractors bite their fingers! Let them offer up their prayers, or hide – if they don't intend to blow the convert's big trumpet, that is.

This dwelling is purpose-built for mid-20th century man, a feat not easy to achieve. It belongs to its time but is probably the only one of its kind; it is a dwelling it would be good to live in.

Le Corbusier was happy. I can tell you also that he was very moved and so were his friends.

Le Corbusier and politics

Although Le Corbusier consistently defended his idea of the city, he had no particular political affiliation. As an architect and town planner, however, he frequently needed to approach what he called 'Authority' for his plans to be put into action. His lack of diplomacy and his approaches to a wide range of people led some of his critics to accuse him of supporting the most extreme political positions of the day. The French government did not recognize his genius in time to commission anything of importance.

One of Le Corbusier's self-portraits.

In his book Art et technique *(1956), Pierre Francastel acknowledges Le Corbusier's influence and his political independence, but describes his built environment as the environment of a concentration camp.*

The influence exercised today by Le Corbusier, the theorist and artist, is immense. In my opinion, our generation will never be able to say enough about him, good or bad.

People have even begun to wonder nowadays if Le Corbusier's theories aren't beginning to resemble the manual of a new type of orthodoxy.

Le Corbusier is a man of order. He perceives order both in terms of the internal logic of a monumental scheme, and of social control. I must stress that Le Corbusier showed admirable dignity at a time when the partisans of a 'new order' were occupying France.... We must never forget that, however mordant his critics may be, his loyalty and honour are not in question.

Le Corbusier's world is the world of the concentration camp. Or, at best, the ghetto. I repeat that there is no question of Le Corbusier being regarded as a mouthpiece for Pétain or Hitler, whose hands and sleeves are stained with mud and blood. It speaks volumes, however, for the evil stalking our era that this monstrous new order should be a perverted version of an ideology that seems to me infinitely threatening to the future of mankind.

In his book De l'architecture *(1938), Louis Hautecoeur compares Le Corbusier's aesthetic to the theories of the 'socialist-communists'.*

A large group of contemporary architects seem to base their aesthetic theories on social needs. There is a correlation between socialist-communist theory and some of these aesthetic theories, between historical materialism and functionalism.... M. Le Corbusier views architecture as a means of satisfying a collection of needs. He knows, for sure, that this definition cannot cover architecture comprehensively, and he therefore expatiates in his books on the beauty of classical proportions.... M. Alex de Senger, in a violent attack...credits M. Le Corbusier with notions like the following: the individual must be eliminated from Bolshevik society; mankind is only a standard element in a vast organization; architecture should also be constructed from standard elements. No more local or national styles, architecture must be as cosmopolitan as the revolutionary spirit.

In the journal Travaux nord-africains *(4 June 1942) Alexander de Senger, a Swiss architect, roundly accuses Le Corbusier of collusion with high finance in a plot to destroy Paris and create a new, subject proletariat.*

Le Corbusier has no hesitation in appealing to the financiers: he has made it known that the destruction of Paris (and other cities) would have wonderful consequences for the cement industry, and for the banks financing the manufacturers of building materials.

The exclusive use of modern building methods will destroy all the craft trades and produce a new proletariat. Thus the non-Bolshevik army will be reduced and the Bolshevik army enlarged. Modern construction destroys the plastic arts, painting and sculpture. It robs man of his soul, reducing him to a geometrical animal. It offers enormous openings to international capital, hugely enlarging its omnipotence. This type of development can be clearly observed in Russia, where state capitalism rules....

This mammoth enterprise is organized on behalf of the International Association for New Construction... directed by a Jew by the name of Siegfried Gedeon [sic], etc., etc....

By the 1950s the Unité d'habitation *had already taken its place as one of the classics of modern architecture. The American historian Peter Blake characterized it as follows:*

The Marseilles structure is all concrete – concrete in its crudest, most brutal form, *le béton brut.* Concrete poured into the simplest form work, to come out looking as rough and virile as rock, deliberately chipped and cracked, full of pebble surfaces here and sea-shell surfaces there, as beautifully textured as the now blackened travertine of the great Roman ruins of Italy and southern France. Next to the Marseilles building, Lever House would look like the latest Cadillac – slick, thin-shelled, soon out of date. Next to the Marseilles building, every other modern 'curtain wall' structure would look as tinny as an oil can, and sure to rust away just as fast. For this massive piece of brute concrete could be of any time: it could be an Egyptian temple of 2000 BC, or a vision of the 21st century....

To many American visitors, in particular, who were used to slick finishes in their buildings, the Marseilles structure seemed to be crude and sloppy. But this is not the case at all; in a sense, this structure is a deliberate affirmation of man in a Machine Art era. The man-made imprint on concrete, according to Corbu, seemed to 'shout at one from all parts of the structure'. Indeed, he stated at the great ceremonial opening of the building that 'it seems to be really possible to consider concrete as a reconstructed stone worthy of being exposed in its natural state'.

Peter Blake
Le Corbusier: Architecture and Form
1960

On 1 September 1965, at the state funeral of Le Corbusier in the Cour Carrée of the Louvre, André Malraux, the minister for cultural affairs, spoke about the architect's genius.

When our government decided to pay the solemn respects of the French people to Le Corbusier, the following telegram arrived from Greece: 'The architects of Greece, in deepest sadness, have decided to send their president to the funeral of Le Corbusier so that he can scatter some earth from the Acropolis on his tomb.'

And yesterday: 'India, where several of Le Corbusier's masterpieces are to be found, including Chandigarh, the capital designed by him, will sprinkle water from the Ganges on his ashes in an act of respectful homage.'

Eternal revenge…. Le Corbusier had famous rivals, some of whom are honouring us with their presence today, some of whom are dead. No one embodied the revolution in architecture as much as he did; no one was insulted so continuously as he was nor bore it so patiently.

In spite of insults, he attained great glory, adulation being addressed more to his work than to the man, who wanted little part of it. After working for many years in the wide corridor of a disused monastery, this man who had designed whole capitals, died in a isolated cabin….

He was a painter, sculptor and, less publicly, a poet. He never did battle for painting, sculpture or poetry, but only for architecture….

His famous phrase 'A house is a machine for living' does not give a clear picture of the man at all; much more appropriate is 'A house should be a casket in which life is led'. A machine for happiness. He always dreamt of cities, and his 'Cités radieuses' always rose out of immense gardens. This agnostic designed the most striking church and monastery to be built this century.

He was of a stature to put up with (often unwittingly) the prophetic theories and exacerbated logic – usually aggressive – that constitute the ferments of this century. A theory either emerges as a masterpiece, or it is forgotten. These, however, brought architects the enormous responsibility that belongs to them today, the conquest of earth's dispositions by the human mind. Le Corbusier changed architecture and architects. This is why he was a major influence in his lifetime…. Le Corbusier was first and foremost the artist who said in 1920: 'Architecture is the intelligent, accurate, magnificent handling of forms assembled in daylight', and, later: 'May our concrete demonstrate that, underneath its rough exterior, our sensibilities are delicate'…. In the name of function and of logic he invented inspiringly arbitrary forms….

It is his work, not his theories, that has made manifest the important, profound relationship between architectural forms….

There is a message from Aalto, who altered the face of Finland, and one from England which says: 'No architect under sixty has escaped his influence'. The Soviet message says: 'Modern architecture has lost its greatest master'.

André Malraux, who paid this tribute to Le Corbusier and his architecture.

The President of the United States says: 'His influence was universal and his works have a durability seldom achieved by any other artist in our history'....

Farewell, master and old friend. Goodnight.

Here is the sacred water of the Ganges and the earth from the Acropolis.

After Le Corbusier's death, many celebrated architects took the opportunity of telling the world of the importance of his work for the future of architecture.

It is difficult to explore all the implications of his work. When he disappeared beyond our immediate field of vision, the impact and weight of his huge personality flashed into my mind. How tragic that he has not had time to realize his fullest potential....

The stability of his life, a huge output of architecture, poetry, invention characterize the work and life of this universal man. He has created a new scale of values, comprehensive enough to enrich the generations to come.

Walter Gropius
10 September 1965

Everyone now recognizes that Le Corbusier was a great architect and a great artist, a true innovator....

For me his profoundest significance lies in the fact that he was a true liberator in the fields of architecture and town planning.

Mies van der Rohe
7 September 1965

Once I had got over the overwhelming news of the death of Le Corbusier, I inevitably began to reflect on his life's work. In fact, it is difficult to decide the field in which this immensely creative and productive man excelled; as an artist, as the pioneer of a new kind of architecture or as a stimulus to the younger generation. Our Corbu, so hardworking and so full of vitality, is dead, but he has not yet stopped (his work lives on).

Marcel Breuer
20 September 1965

These joined hands were drawn by Le Corbusier.

Statement

*Le Corbusier (below)
provided a constant
written commentary on his
own progress. In July 1965,
at the age of seventy-seven,
a few weeks before he died,
he issued his last statement
in a small book,* Mise
au point.

Thought alone can be handed down.
Over the years, people struggle and
strive, by their own great efforts
acquiring a certain capital. But all this
individual endeavour, this capital, this
hard-won experience will vanish. The
one sure rule of life is death. Nature
puts an end to all activity with death.
Thought alone, the outcome of labour,
can be handed down. The days pass,
as they pass, as life passes....

When I was young I had direct
contact with the weight of things.
The weight and durability of materials.
Then with people: the different
strengths of people, resistance of men
and resistance to men. I lived in their
company, that was my life. And
proposing bold solutions to the weight
of materials...but it lasted! And
knowing that people were like this or
like that. Sometimes I was amazed and
even stupefied. Recognizing, admitting,
having seen, seeing.... Playing my
humble part come wind or rain....

I am seventy-seven years old and my
doctrine can be summed up as follows:
it is essential to take part in life. By
which I mean that it is essential to
behave with modesty and accuracy,
with precision. The only atmosphere
in which artistic creation can be born
is an atmosphere of regularity, modesty,
consistency, perseverance.

I have already stated somewhere that
constancy defines life, because constancy
is natural and productive. To be
constant you have to be modest, and
you have to persevere. Constancy bears
witness to courage and inner strength,
qualifications for the very nature
of existence.

I am an ass, but an ass with an eye.
I am talking about the eye of an ass
capable of experiencing feelings. I am an
ass with an instinct for proportion. I am

and shall remain unrepentantly visual. What is beautiful is beautiful.

Since I built my first house at the age of seventeen and a half, I have pursued my wanderer's way through problems and catastrophes and, from time to time, success. Now I am seventy-seven and my name is known all over the world. My discoveries and ideas are sometimes shared, but there are still detractors and obstructions in my way. My response? I have always been active and I shall remain so. My investigations have always aimed at the poetry that exists in our hearts. I am a visual person who works with his eyes and hands; what motivates me chiefly is the physical appearance of things. All is in everything: cohesion, coherence, unity. Architecture and town planning combined: a single problem to be addressed by a single profession.

I am not a revolutionary; I am reticent, I do not meddle with things that do not concern me. But the elements are revolutionary, events are revolutionary, these things must be considered calmly, from afar....

Away from noise and crowds, in my lair (I am a solitary, in reality, and have even compared myself with conviction to an ass), I have for the last fifty years been studying the 'little man' and his wife and children. One concern has been uppermost in my mind: to make the family sacred, to make a temple of the family home. Once I had thought of this everything changed. A cubic centimetre of housing was worth its weight in gold, so much happiness did it represent. With such a perception of dimension and destiny a temple can be made to fit the family – leave aside the cathedrals that were built... in the past; you can do it because your heart will be in it....

The task is to take on places and premises. This is the task of the 'constructors' . And the 'constructors' represent this new profession that links the engineer and the architect, the left and right hand of the art of building, in tireless, fraternal dialogue.

These circumstances could not, however, lead to the dwelling becoming a temple for the family. Boxes for rent were created, and livelihoods made from them. The perception of architecture was unsound because there was no accurate definition of what it should be: no one stated that architecture should create places or abodes for living, working and spending free time; free time should be spent 'in natural conditions', i.e. under the strictest orders of the sun, our incontestable master, since day and night follow one another and regulate the sequence of our activities....

People must be rediscovered. The straight line linking the fundamental laws – biology, nature, cosmos – must be rediscovered. Like the sea's horizon, this straight line can be inflected....

This has been running through my head, taking shape very gradually, during a lifetime lived at breakneck speed; I shall arrive at life's end without even noticing it.

Mise au point
July 1965

THE FONDATION LE CORBUSIER

The Fondation Le Corbusier was set up in 1968 in accordance with the architect's wishes. It is housed in the Villas La Roche and Jeanneret and has charitable status.

The foundation is Le Corbusier's sole legatee. It holds and assumes all ethical and patrimonial rights and responsibilities connected with the architect's architectural, artistic and literary works.

It holds the major part of archives for Le Corbusier: drawings, studies, plans, written and photographic material. It also possesses many examples of his artistic output in a number of different media – drawings, paintings, designs for tapestries, collages, as well as most of the sculpture he produced with Joseph Savina. The foundation inherited Le Corbusier's collection of books. It is responsible for preserving this bequest.

It also administers a library devoted to Le Corbusier and his work. This is accessible to anyone interested, to students, architects, historians and researchers. It welcomes visitors to the Villa La Roche.

The foundation organizes exhibitions, meetings and conferences. It collaborates in the organization of other events, primarily by the loan of works from the collection. When requested, it advises the owners of buildings designed by Le Corbusier on their maintenance and renovation.

It maintains close relations with other organizations in France and abroad that are interested in the work of Le Corbusier. It maintains permanent contact with governments or government departments facing problems with modern architecture and its conservation.

LE CORBUSIER'S BUILDINGS

IN FRANCE: PARIS

—, Maison du Peuple (1926). 29 Rue des Cordelières
—, Villa Planeix (1924–7). 24bis, Boulevard Massena
—, Salvation Army hostel (1929–33). 12 Rue Cantagrel
—, Atelier Ozenfant (1923–4). 53 Avenue Reille
—, Pavillon Suisse (1929–33). Cité Universitaire, 7 Boulevard Jourdan
—, Pavillon du Brésil (1957–9, with Lucio Costa). Cité Universitaire, 7 Boulevard Jourdan
—, Villas La Roche and Jeanneret (1923–5). 8–10, Square du Docteur-Blanche
—, Apartment block (1933–5). 24 Rue Nungesser-et-Coli

IN THE PARIS REGION

Boulogne-sur-Seine
—, Villa Ternisien (1923–6). 5 Allée des Pins
—, Villa Lipchitz (1924–5). 9 Allée des Pins
—, Villa Miestchaninoff (1923–6). 7 Rue des Arts
—, Villa Cook (1926–7). 6 Rue Denfert-Rochereau
La Celle-Saint-Cloud

—, Weekend Henfel house (1935). 49 Avenue du Chesnay
Neuilly-sur-Seine
—, Jaoul houses (1951–5). 81bis Rue de Longchamp
Poissy
—, Villa Savoye (1929–31). 82 Chemin de Villiers
Vaucresson
—, Villa Besnus (1923). 85 Boulevard de la République
—, Villa Stein 'Les Terrasses' (1927–8). 17 Rue du Professeur-Victor-Pauchet

OUTSIDE THE PARIS REGION

Bordeaux-Pessac
—, Quartier Frugès (1924–7). Avenue Henri-Frugès
Briey
—, *Unité d'habitation* (1956–63). Rue du Dr-Giry.
Eveux-sur-l'Arbresle (20 km from Lyons)
—, Monastery at La Tourette (1953–9)
Firminy (10 km from Saint-Etienne)
—, Cultural centre (1955–65), sports centre (1955–68), *Unité d'habitation* (1959–67, with André Wogenscky and Fernand Gardien)
La Palmyre (Les Mathes, 20 km from Royan)
—, Villa Le Sextant (1935)

Marseilles
—, *Unité d'habitation* (1945–52). 280 Boulevard Michelet
Mulhouse (12 km outside)
—, The lock at Kembs Niffer, on the Rhône-Rhine canal (1960–2)
Nantes-Rezé
—, *Unité d'habitation* (1953–5), Boulevard Le Corbusier
Podensac (35 km from Bordeaux)
—, Water tower (1917)
Le Pradet (7 km from Toulon)
—, Villa de Mandrot (1930–1)
Ronchamp (20 km from Belfort)
—, pilgrimage church of Notre-Dame-du-Haut (1950–5)
Roquebrune-Cap-Martin
—, Cabanon Le Corbusier (1951–2)
—, Tomb of Le Corbusier and his wife Yvonne (1957), cemetery
Saint-Dié
—, Duval factory (1946–50). 88 Avenue de Robache

IN OTHER PARTS OF THE WORLD

Argentina
La Plata
—, Currutchet house (1949). 320 Boulevard 53

Belgium
Antwerp
—, Guiette house (1926–7). 32 Avenue des Peupliers

Brazil
Rio de Janeiro
—, Ministry of Education (1936, with Oscar Niemeyer and Lucio Costa)

Germany
Charlottenburg, Berlin
—, *Unité d'habitation* (1956–8), Heilsberger Dreieck 143
Stuttgart
—, Two houses in the Weissenhof (1927)

India
Chandigarh (Punjab)
—, Plan of the city (1942–63), Courts of Justice (1955), Secretariat (1958), Parliament Building (1962), museum (1964–8), School of Art and Architecture (1964–9)

Ahmedabad (Gujarat)
—, headquarters of the wool weaver's association (1954), Villa Sarabhai (1956), Villa Shodan (1956), Museum (1958)

Italy
In 1977, twenty-two years after Le Corbusier's death, a pavilion was built in Bologna to the same design as the Pavillon de l'esprit nouveau *in the 1925 exhibition, the original one having been demolished immediately after the exhibition.*

Bologna
—, Pavillon de l'esprit nouveau (1925, reconstructed in 1977 under the direction of José Oubrerie and G. Gresleri).

Japan
Tokyo
—, Museum of Western Art (1959)

Russia
Moscow
—, Centrosoyus (Central statistical office) (1929–35), 35–41 Miastnitzkaya

Switzerland
La Chaux-de-Fonds
—, Villa Fallet (1905–7). 1 Chemin de Pouillerel
—, Villa Jacquemet (1908–9). 8 Chemin de Pouillerel
—, Villa Stotzer (1908–9). 6 Chemin de Pouillerel
—, Villa Jeanneret (1912). 12 Chemin de Pouillerel
—, Scala cinema (1916). 32 Rue de la Senne
—, Villa Schwob (1916–7). 167 Rue du Doubs
Corseaux-Vevey
—, Jeanneret house, the 'Petite Maison' (1924–5). 21 Route de Lavaux
Geneva
—, Clarté flats (1930–2). 2 Rue Saint-Laurent
Le Locle
—, Villa Favre-Jacquot (1912). 6 Rue des Billodes
Zurich
—, Le Corbusier-Heidi Weber Centre (1963–7). Höschgasse

Tunisia
Carthage
—, Villa Baiseau (1928–31), Sainte-Monique

United States of America
Cambridge (Mass.)
—, Carpenter Center for the Visual Arts (1962–3). 24 Quincy Street, Harvard University

THE WRITTEN WORKS OF LE CORBUSIER

Aircraft, 1935

L'Almanach d'architecture moderne, 1925

L'Art décoratif d'aujourd'hui, 1925. (*The Decorative Art of Today*, trans. James I. Dunnett, 1987)

Après le cubisme (with Amédée Ozenfant), 1918

L'Atelier de la recherche patiente, 1960

Des canons, des munitions? Merci! Des logis S.V.P., 1938

La Charte d'Athènes, 1943

The Chapel at Ronchamp, trans. Jacqueline Cullen, 1957

Complete works (translated A. J. Dakin and William B. Gleckman): *1910–65*, 1967; *1910–29*, 1929; *1929–34*, 1935; *1934–8*, 1939; *1938–46*, 1947; *1946–52*, 1953; *1952–7*, 1957; *1957–65*, 1965; *1965–9*, 1970

Croisade, ou le Crépuscule des académies, 1933

Dessins, 1968

Destin de Paris, 1941

Deuxième clavier de couleurs, 1959

Entretien avec les étudiants des écoles d'architecture, 1943. (*Le Corbusier Talks with Students from the Schools of Architecture*, trans. Pierre Chase, 1961)

Etude sur le mouvement d'art décoratif en Allemagne, 1912

Le Corbusier. Carnets, 1981–2

Le Corbusier dessins, 1968

La Maison des hommes (with François de Pierrefeu), 1942. (*The Home of Man*, trans. Clive Entwhistle and Gordon Holt, 1948)

Une Maison, un palais, 1928

Manière de penser l'urbanisme, 1946

Mise au point, 1966

Le Modulor, 1950. (*The Modulor*, trans. Peter de Francia and Anna Bostock, 1954)

Modulor 2. La Parole est aux usagers, 1955 (*Modulor 2. Let the User Speak Next*, trans. Peter de Francia and Anna Bostock, 1958)

La Peinture moderne (with Amédée Ozenfant), 1925

Une petite maison, 1954. (trans. Elizabeth Dow, 1995)

Les Plans de Paris, 1956

Le Poème de l'angle droit, 1955

Poésie sur Alger, 1950

Précisions sur un état présent de l'architecture et de l'urbanisme, 1930

Premier Clavier de couleurs, 1931

Quand les cathédrales étaient blanches. Voyage aux pays des timides, 1937. (*When the Cathedrals were White*, trans. Francis E. Hyslop, 1947)

Sur les quatre routes, 1941. (*The Four Routes*, trans. Dorothy Todd, 1947)

Les Trois Etablissements humains (in collaboration), 1945

Urbanisme, 1925. (*The City of Tomorrow and its Planning*, trans. Frederick Etchells, 1929)

L'Urbanisme est une clef, 1955

Vers une architecture, 1923. (*Towards a New Architecture*, trans. Frederick Etchells, 1927)

La Ville radieuse, 1935. (*The Radiant City*, trans. Pamela Knight, Eleanor Levieux, Derek Coltman, 1967)

Le Voyage d'Orient, 1966. (*Journey to the East*, trans. Ivan Zaknic and Nicole Pertuiset, 1987)

FURTHER READING

Baker, G. H., *Le Corbusier: The Creative Search*, 1996

Blake, Peter, *Le Corbusier: Architecture and Form*, 1960

Choay, Françoise, *Le Corbusier*, 1960

Curtis, William J. R., *Le Corbusier: Ideas and Forms*, 1986

Evanson, N., *Chandigarh*, 1966

Franchetti Pardo, Vittorio, *Le Corbusier: The Life and Work of the Artist*, trans. Pearl Sanders, 1971

Gardiner, Stephen, *Le Corbusier*, 1974

Jencks, Charles, *Le Corbusier and the Tragic View of Architecture*, 1973

Jordan, Robert Furneaux, *Le Corbusier*, 1972

Palazzolo, Carlo, and Riccardo Voa (eds.), *In the Footsteps of Le Corbusier*, 1991

Raeburn, M., and V. Wilson (eds.), *Le Corbusier: Architect of the Century*, 1987

Taylor, B. B., *The City of Refuge*, 1987

Turner, P. V., *The Education of Le Corbusier: A Study of the Development of Le Corbusier's Thought, 1900–20*, 1977

Von Moos, Stanislaus, *Le Corbusier: Elements of a Synthesis*, 1979

Walden, Russell (ed.), *The Open Hand: Essays on Le Corbusier*, 1977

LIST OF ILLUSTRATIONS

All works are by Le Corbusier unless stated otherwise.

FLC: documents, photographs and works of art (drawings, paintings, sculpture, tapestry) in the Fondation Le Corbusier, Paris.

COVER

Front Ronchamp. Photograph Marvin Trachtenberg
Spine *Unité d'habitation*, Marseilles. Model of the framework, 1946. FLC
Back Villa La Roche, Paris. Photograph. FLC

OPENING

1–7 Lithographs taken from the *Poème de l'angle droit*, 1955
9 Notre-Dame-du-Haut, Ronchamp. Photograph

CHAPTER 1

10 *Landscape of the Jura* (detail). Gouache, c. 1905. FLC (2204)
11 *Crow*. Drawing. FLC
12a Engraved watchcase, 1902–3. Photograph. FLC
12b Charles-Edouard Jeanneret (right) in the Jura with Léon Perrin (left). Photograph. FLC
13a *Flowers and Leaves*. Watercolour, 1905 or 1906. FLC (2206)
13b Charles-Edouard Jeanneret (on the pedestal) with his brother Albert and their parents. Photograph, 1889. FLC
14a Charles L'Eplattenier. Photograph
14b Villa Fallet. Photograph, c. 1907. FLC
15 Siena cathedral. Watercolour, 1907. FLC (6055)
16 Fiesole. Watercolour, 1907. FLC (2856)
17a The Carthusian monastery at Ema, near Florence. Drawing, 1907. FLC
17b The citadel at Nuremberg. Watercolour, 1908. FLC (2031)
18 *Auguste Perret*. Drawing, 1924. FLC (2453)
19 Block of flats built by the Perret brothers in 1903 at 25bis, Rue Franklin, Paris. Photograph

CHAPTER 2

20 Self-portrait. Watercolour, 1917. FLC (5131)
21 Shell. Drawing, 1932. FLC
22a and 22b Villa Jaquemet. Drawings and photograph, c. 1910. FLC
23a and 22b Villa Stotzer. Drawings and photograph, c. 1910. FLC
24a House in the country. Drawing, undated. FLC (6082)
24b Tarnovo, Bulgaria. Drawing, 1911. FLC (2496)
24–5 Charles-Edouard Jeanneret by the Parthenon. Photograph, 1911. FLC
25 Map showing the itinerary of the journey in Asia Minor. Drawing, 1911. FLC
26–7 Istanbul and the Parthenon. Drawings made on the journey to the East (details), 1908 and 1911. FLC (2454, 1784, notebook no. 3, 1911, 2384, 1941, 6111)
28a and 28b Villa Favre-Jacot. Photographs. FLC
28–9 Villa Jeanneret. Photograph. FLC
30–1 Villa Schwob. Contract, photographs and detail of the plan. FLC
32 The basic unit of the Dom-ino system. Drawing, 1914. FLC (19209)
32–3 Group of terrace houses built on the Dom-ino system. Drawing, 1915, FLC (1931)
33 Charles-Edouard (left) with Albert (right) and their parents in the Villa Jeanneret at La Chaux-de-Fonds. Photograph, c. 1918. FLC

CHAPTER 3

34 Villa La Roche, Paris. Photograph
35 Open-hand motif. Drawing. FLC
36 Maison Loucheur, *Maison d'artiste* and *La ferme radieuse*. Drawings, 1929, 1922 and 1938. FLC (18253, 30198, 28619)
36–7 Houses in series. Drawing, 1919, in *Vers une architecture*, 1923
37 Le Corbusier with Yvonne. Photograph, c. 1935. FLC
38 *The Mantelpiece*. Painting, 1918. FLC (134)
39a *Three Bottles*. Painting, 1921. FLC (144)
39b Amédée Ozenfant, Albert Jeanneret and Charles-Edouard Jeanneret. Photograph, c. 1918. FLC
40l Shell. Drawing, 1932. FLC

CHAPTER 4

CHAPTER 5

DOCUMENTS

INDEX

━━━━━━━━━━━━━━━━

ACKNOWLEDGMENTS

The author would like to thank all those who have helped him to understand the life and work of Le Corbusier, and in particular Roger Aujame, Michel Bataille, Maurice Besset, Abbé Bolle Reddat, Françoise de Franclieu, Giuliano Gresleri, Maurice Jardot, Charlotte Perriand, Robert Rebutato, Roland Simounet, Evelyne Tréhin and André Wogenscky. He also owes a debt of gratitude to the memory of Eugène Claudius Petit, François Mathey and Jean Prouvé.

The publishers would like to thank: the Fondation Le Corbusier, and in particular Evelyne Tréhin and Holy Raveloarisoa; and Bernard Piens for his valuable contribution to the picture research.

━━━━━━━━━━━━━━━━

PHOTO CREDITS

━━━━━━━━━━━━━━━━

TEXT CREDITS

Grateful acknowledgment is made for use of material from the following works:
(pp. 147–8) Peter Blake, *Le Corbusier,* 1960; copyright © Peter Blake, 1960; reprinted with permission of Aitken & Stone Ltd, London. (pp. 119, 125–6, 134–7) Le Corbusier, *The Decorative Art of Today,* trans. James I. Dunnett, London, 1987; reprinted by permission of the translator. (pp. 124–5, 126–7, 128, 130–2) Le Corbusier, *Towards a New Architecture,* trans. Frederick Etchells, 1927; reprinted by permission of Butterworth-Heinemann Ltd, Oxford.

Jean Jenger
served in the French ministry of culture
for many years, first in the department with
responsibility for the schools of art and architecture,
then in the department dealing with new public
buildings. He then became assistant director of
the Caisse Nationale des Monuments Historiques,
and was subsequently its deputy director for
architecture. From 1978 to 1986 he was
in charge of setting up the Musée d'Orsay for
the French government. In 1971 he became
administrator of the Fondation
Le Corbusier and its president from 1982
to 1988 and again from 1990 to 1992.
He is the author of *Orsay, de la gare
au musée* (1986) and of *Le Corbusier,
un autre regard* (1990).

Translated from the French by Caroline Beamish

Series manager, Harry N. Abrams, Inc.: Eve Sinaiko

Library of Congress Catalog Card Number: 96–83348

ISBN 0–8109–2880–9

Printed and bound in Italy by Editoriale Libraria, Trieste